A PASTOR'S INTRODUCTION TO CHURCH ADMINISTRATION

A Pastor's Introduction to Church Administration

Administering the 21st Century Church Effectively

Jeremy W. Odom

Big O Publishing Group

© 2016

Ordering Information:

Special discounts are available on quantity purchases by corporations, associations, educators, and others. For details, contact the publisher at Big O Publishing Group, 431 5th Street, Natchitoches, LA 71457.

U.S. trade bookstores and wholesalers: Please make contact with Big O Publishing Group via email sales@bigopublishinggroup.com.

I dedicate this book with gratitude to my pastor Dr. Mitchell Charles Herndon, Sr. for his love, leadership and encouragement to my ministry; who along with my many comrades in the Gospel Ministry made it possible to bring this idea to fruition.

Contents

What Exactly is Church Administration

There is a question that I have been approached by several pastors and ministers that I am praying that can be answered through the contents of this chapter— What exactly is church administration? For a more direct answer to this question, I refer to Dr. Charles A. Tidwell who is a professor of Church Administration at Southwestern Baptist Theological Seminary in Fort Worth, Texas.

Church administration is the leadership which equips the church to be the church and to do the work of the church. It is the guidance provided by church leaders as they lead the church to use its spiritual, human, physical, and financial resources to move the church toward reaching its objectives and fulfilling its avowed purpose. It is enabling the children of God who comprise the church to become and to do what they can become and do, by God's grace.

Dr. John H. Tyson considers it ironic that most of us spend more time in our ministry doing church administration than any other single task of ministry although it is one chore which we all loathe. Dr. Tyson goes on to point out that many of us spend one-third of our ministry time doing administration while some pastors claim to spend up to 60% of their time.

However, as both Dr. Tidwell and Dr. Tyson attempt to do, I am going to expound on this thing called church administration. Tyson warns that no matter how beautiful we preach or how soundly we teach that if we fail in the area of administration and leadership, we will fail in other areas of our ministry as well. He contends that an important part of Paul's point in both Romans 12 and 1 Corinthians 12 is that all of the gifts are necessary for the healthy functioning of the body of Christ—including administration.

On the most basic level, we cannot lead if we aren't present at the right time, in the right place, with the right equipment. If we cannot organize on that basic level, we cannot lead, simply because we are not present and equipped to lead. Good administration is inseparable from good leadership. The author George Hunter noted that administration is a subcategory of leadership: the higher your level of leadership, the higher your level of administration; but leaders always administrate on the level of their leadership. Leadership without effective administration is not leadership; it is philosophy.

Many first-pastors are surprised when they discover that the job description and expectations of the pastor differ from what he or she had thought. Most pastors operate under the premise that when they accepted their calling from the Lord, it was only to preach and not to run a business. Several African American pastors in particular look forward to grazing the pulpit on Sunday after Sunday while loathing the tasks of budgeting, staff management, and the countless meetings. As a result, many of these pastors become better preachers than they are administrators.

Church administration is coming to fruition with more attention being focused on the matter since 1950. Church leaders and members alike are showing a growing sensitivity to the need for the work of the church to be done decently and in order.

Needs for Good Church Administration

There are several needs which call attention to the importance of good church administration and to the necessity of an adequate conceptual approach. Some of these needs are rather apparent.

A Church Needs Good Administration

As a living organism, the church is a basic unit constituted to carry on the activities of its life by means of parts separate in function but mutually dependent. Such an organism requires administration—*good* administration—if it is to be very effective.

A church is of God and people.—There is an essential partnership between God and persons in the life and work of a church. Church administration concerns itself with presenting the human element in the partnership equation as a disciplined, orderly, purposeful instrument to be directed and used of God as He sees fit. W. T. Conner writes "The Lord can cut more timber with a sharp axe than with a dull one." Church administration attempts to sharpen that axe.

Church resources are limited.—Church administration concerns itself with the overall guidance provided by church leaders as they utilize the spiritual, human, physical, and financial resources of the church to enable the church to move toward fulfilling its purpose and objectives. Church administration offers good management for a church's limited resources.

Churches are experiencing sagging influence and lagging pace.—The well-documented decline of the influence of churches on society, the continuing decline of participation in many churches, and other signs of the times indicate that churches are losing ground. Like Christianity, church administration has yet to have been tried and found wanting. Gross inefficiencies in the administrative affairs of the church glare to the observant church member, with resulting ineffectiveness.

Many churches have been administered poorly.— Henry Ford took it as sign of the reality of "Deity" that the church had survived at all noting that no other enterprise run so poorly could stay in business. It would be the concerned church administrator who asks "How long shall we go on presuming on God?"

Churches Deserve Good Administration

A church is part of the cause which is just and right. It is the instrument of God. It is under the lordship of Christ. It is relating the gospel in all its fullness to all the needs of the people.

A church proclaims the good news and witnesses.— This proclaiming and witnessing is not only within the confines of the church walls but beyond those walls wherever receptive people may be found. Good administrative leadership provides the best guidance available to the leaders in this work of a church along with their co-workers and those who are the objects of their efforts.

A church educates and nurtures. A church is learning, teaching, educating, and nurturing. A church desires to make some significant things happen and therefore is increasingly interested in learning that results in responsible living. Good church administration can lead in the discovery and development of effective leaders in learning and nurturing.

A church ministers to persons in need.—The number of persons in need continues to spiral because their needs proliferate at a progressively faster rate. A church is a ministering organism which attempts to minister unselfishly knowing that such attempt merits the best guidance a church can muster. Good administration is able to provide much of this guidance.

A church worships God.—A church experiences His presence in an encounter which is life-changing and empowering. Good church administration can help significantly in multiplying and enhancing the occasions of worshipping encounter.

Church Leaders Need Help in Administration

Ministers and other church leaders often find ourselves subject to increasing demands for administrative effectiveness and are more and more caught up in admin-istration. Some ministers actually enjoy being busy with administrative work which requires more knowledge and skills in *doing things* than in *developing persons*. However, once these leaders move up to developing people rather than doing things, they are seldom content to revert to their former state.

Church leaders feel the impact of change pace.—The world has become more complicated in many ways for the church leader. The alert church leader is more aware of the many needs of persons than in previous times being more conscious of the need for response from the church. It is imperative that the responses from the church be more and more sensitive.

Working with people heightens leaders' tensions.—Democratic participation demands keen administrative insights. Dr. Tidwell explains in his writings that many leaders' tensions are heightened because they are happier doing what they can do alone rather than having to involve others in their efforts. Unfortunately, administration of a democracy calls for more than one person can do alone thereby requiring the minister to work with people in order to be effective.

Improved leadership in nonchurch sectors affects the church.—The quality of leadership in other than church organizations has generally, though not universally, improved. There is a higher educational level among church members which reflects that of the general population. Many church members expect leadership intensity and quality of effort in the church comparable to that which they work in their jobs out-side the church.

The pressures produced by improved leadership out-side the church may be somewhat offset by the possibilities of transferring some of the good concepts and skills from members' occupational experiences to the area of church leadership. The church leader must be adept in administration to make the most of this po-tential. The minister can never afford to stop improving his ability to lead in deploying leadership resources of church members.

Churches are doing more things with and for more people.—Church programs are multiplying. Church organizations are growing more complex. Church members have heightened expectations of their leaders. Leadership is becoming more and more intricate, both in its artistic and in its scientific aspects. A thorough working knowledge of good church administration, accompanied by the attitudes and skills to make possi-ble the use of this knowledge, may be the best, most helpful option for the minister. Such knowledge, atti-tudes, and skills enable the leader to multiply personal energies through others and rise above the avalanche of responsibilities.

Church Leaders Need an Administrative Style of Leadership

Church leaders need to discover, accept, and develop an administrative style of leadership. The need is not a new one. Neither is the approach to the remedy. Both are apparent in history at least as far back as the Exodus. The lessons which Jethro taught Moses rested on the premise that in order for leaders to endure and to get the work done, they must lead others to bear the burden as well. This is the meaning of an administrative style of leadership.

Practical Application Exercises

1. Interview three ministers who are currently serving in churches.
   a. Write down this information from each interview:
      i. Estimate of the proportion or percentage of work time each spends on administration.
      ii. Activities each lists as illustrative of their individual administrative work.

2. Prepare a summation of 1,000 words or fewer detailing the need for effective church administration.

3. Write a paragraph in 750 words or slightly less, in which you define church administration.

Recommended Resources for Further Study

Powers, Bruce P. ed., Church Administration Handbook. B&H Publishing Group, 2008. (ISBN 978-0-8054-4490-2)

Welch, Jack, Winning. Harper Collins, 2013. (ISBN 978-0-062-27401-4)

Welch, Robert E., Church Administration: Creating Efficiency for Effective Ministry. B&H Publishing Group, 2011. (ISBN 978-1-433-67377-1)

The Pastoral Staff

With the overwhelming growth of new ministers seeking pastorates without formal seminary training, it is important to address the Pastoral/Ministerial staff when dealing with the leadership of the Christian Church. I have seen great, strong pastors enter into their eternal reward and because there was no structure in place to outline the role of the ministers on staff, the Church suffered greatly. I feel that is important for Pastor to have a good staff in place to aid him in his pastoral ministry primarily because it is warranted.

Pastors are quick to introduce and show off their Associate Ministers but it should be understood that Associate Ministers are not automatically considered a part of the pastoral staff. One writer classified Associate Ministers as simply "catch-22 church members." They hold no true authority in the Church but are not only regular members of the local Church because they have been set aside for the Ministry of the Gospel.

It is imperative that we clearly define the role of each individual who will play a role in the administration of the Church. I have even heard horror stories of seminaries that do not even teach Church Administration in their classes turning an overwhelming amount of preachers loose without the adequate understanding of how to fulfill their role as Pastor in their new Parish.

When dealing with these extra servants, one would be wise to consider the following questions when preparing to define roles:

1. What is the role and purpose of that "other guy who helps the pastor sometimes" on the staff at the church?
2. How does his ministry relate to the total program and purpose of the church?
3. How is he different from the Senior Pastor who preaches from the pulpit every Sunday?
4. What is their relationship?

Unfortunately, these and many questions have gone unaddressed for far too long in our churches. While many churches have carefully planned and plotted job descriptions for everyone from the Sunday School class pianist to the church bus driver, they have neglected any extended or Biblical treatment of church staff relationships. Countless books have been written on the position and practice of pastoring. Some articles and materials are available that deal with the Director of Christian Education, Youth Pastor and Assistant Pastor although written from the work load perspective. However, only a few are written and available concerning personal relationships, authority, and the call of God in relation to the various members of the church staff. Much that has been written to that regard tends to hedge in the matter of biblical relationships within the staff.

Therefore, another question remains to be addressed. What order should the various pastoral staff positions be filled? When the church moves beyond a single pastor, which assisting position should be added next?

A Clarification

No matter how many churches you survey, you must conclude that each is unique in structure, needs, outreach and size. No two churches will require exactly the same staff, nor do they make the same demands upon that staff. Historically, churches have adopted one of three general methods of meeting their staff needs. These three methods are *hiring a single pastor, hiring a sectional multiple staff,* and *hiring a vocational multiple staff.* A fourth, more recent, variation involves a *single pastoral leader with a team of laymen who are highly trained and qualified to perform "pastoral level" ministry as volunteers.*

Single Pastor

Because of size and resources, the vast majority of churches in America have and continue to meet their staffing needs by calling only one man. That one man assumes responsibility for the total program of the church. The church rises or falls with his care. He must be an authority on everything from preaching to leading three-year-olds in singing. With a part- or full-time secretary and perhaps a building custodian under his direct management, he often carries the entire load of the church.

The Sectional Multiple Staff

Many larger churches must call more than one man to perform the necessary tasks related to the worship, education, and outreach of their people. One method of selecting such a staff is what may be called the sectional method. In such cases, the key leader of the staff is the pastor, who is also the expositor of the Word. He may gather other men around him who serve as his assistants. These individuals are considered to be his helpers. Their primary function is to extend the ministry of the pastor by doing those jobs which he cannot do for lack of time or primary interest.

The Pastor will sometimes refer to them as "my assistant" "my associate" and "my youth man," and they assume the role of subordinates, functioning as something less than full-fledged pastors. These are usually short-term staff members who are gaining experience and prestige in preparation for a full-fledged pastorate. While they learn, they minister in the church by leading the youth, directing the choir, doing office work, or running pastoral errands. The very term "assistant" assumes eventually taking over the "boss's" job or moving to another church to become "the" pastor.

Another form of the sectional method involves a youth pastor, children's worker, senior citizen's pastor, director of women's ministries, or some combination of these. The effort is to hire staff members to direct or lead certain groups within the church. This method sections the church off by age groups. A high degree of isolation is possible in which the youth and adult ministries are unrelated to one another except through the pastor. Under such an arrangement, the pastor is the undisputed head, and the assistant, youth, children's, senior citizens', or women's ministries pastor is viewed as a hired professional, much like a secretary or custodian who does his or her job as directed.

The sectional multiple staff divides the church into groups comprised of people of the same age. As a specialist, each member of the staff ministers to a particular section of the church such as youth, children, or adults. In the medium sized or large church, the preaching pastor normally leads ministries involving primarily adults. These staff members have assumed various titles including assistant pastor, youth pastor, pastor of Christian education; but their basic function is to be a direct subordinate of the pastor, extending his ministry in one specific section of the church.

The Vocational Multiple Staff

Some larger churches have a grasped a third method of procedure in selecting and organizing a multiple staff. In this approach, each member of the staff functions in a particular vocation or call of God. Each staff member is a specialist in a particular field such as education, preaching/worship, counseling, evangelism, visitation, music/worship, or counseling. He conducts his ministry vertically through the entire congregation from the very youngest to the oldest member. The church is not sectioned off by age as in the previous method; rather, they work with a specific aspect of the ministry as it relates to every age, sex, peer group, or interest group.

The members of the staff are servants of the congregation—not primarily subordinates of one man. They all share a common call of God and are held in esteem by the congregation, sharing in the responsibilities and decisions as under-shepherds of the Lord Jesus Christ. Each must be sound in doctrinal position, competent in his field, and compatible with his fellow staff members.

Although one pastor must serve as administrative head, the rest of the staff is no less important to the entire ministry of the Church. Their influence is felt throughout the church. As a team, they conduct the affairs of the church and promote its well-being and spiritual growth. The vocational multiple staff is consistent with biblical teaching and functionally beneficial.

As a church grows, it passes through various stages where additional paid staff is needed either to lead new ministry areas or to concentrate larger blocks of leadership time and energy on specific age groups. It would be normal and consistent with the vocational approach to add pastors within the responsibility of worship/leadership, education/edification, and outreach/missions.

As a church surpasses an attendance of 600-800, it would be helpful to add a pastor of worship and music to the senior pastor's area of direct supervision. The pastor of worship/praise would also work vocationally with all ages. Some would make a strong case for the worship/music area being a fourth vocational division on the same administrative level as the senior pastor, pastor of education, and pastor of outreach although this author would not. As the church grows, a pastor of counseling ministries and pastor of church business might also be added to the senior pastor's immediate ministry team.

With the demands and needs of a congregation of 800-1,000, a church would normally consider a youth pastor to the educational area of the church. By the time a church approaches 2,000, the pastor of education might have four age-group pastors on his team for adult, youth, children's, and pre-school ministries.

The outreach area of vocational ministry could expand to include staff church planters and missionaries, as well as specific full-time special ministry pastors.

The Biblical Basis of a Vocational Multiple Staff

A consideration of the vocational multiple staff concept from the Bible is essential if one is to move beyond tradition and secular management concepts. Three vantage points could be utilized.

1. Vocational staff can be seen as a cure for potential divisions in the church as found by implication in 1 Corinthians chapters one through three.

2. A vocational staff is compatible with the practices of the early church in the Pastoral Epistles.
3. The vocational multiple staff fits the concepts of "gifted men" in Ephesians 4.

Vocational Staff: A Potential to Cure Church Divisions

The carnality of the citizens of Corinth was exemplified by divisions within the Corinthian church which were centered on particular men who affected a section of the church. A strong division existed inside of the Corinthian church despite its external oneness. For the Corinthians to say that they were of Paul, or Cephas, or Apollos (1 Cor. 3:4) was similar to claiming a sort of "sectional ministry" for each of these men. Paul corrected this view by explaining that each of the men ministered to the whole church in some particular spiritual gift, capacity, or vocation (1 Cor. 3:5-8; 10-20).

Paul's plea to the Corinthians is simply that they should not exalt one man above another or follow one because he had certain abilities or appealed to one interest group or age group more than another. Each one [all being members of the church] was a servant of God called to minister to the entire church (1 Cor. 3:20-23). The church's duty therefor was to accept each one because he fulfilled his vocation and participated effectively in planting, watering, and cultivating.

Vocational Staff: The Pattern in the Pastoral Epistles

The pastoral epistles instruct the young pastors to minister to every age group, interest group, social group, and sex. In Titus 2, Paul admonished Pastor Titus to "instruct" the congregation through the classifications of old men, old women, young men, young women, servants and masters. Likewise, he (Paul) exhorted Timothy to a transgenerational ministry of his pastoral role of exhortation and rebuke (1 Tim. 5:1). These are the responsibilities of all who assume the role of pastor. It must have been as true in Paul's day as in ours that some men felt more at home with one group than with another. However, the instruction reveals that each pastor must not yield to his particular likes and dislikes. He must cut across the age group sections of the church to perform his ministry. It would appear that the teaching of the Pastoral Epistles is inclined toward a vocational ministry rather than a sectional ministry.

Vocational Staff and "Gifted Men"

In Ephesians 4:11, the division of gifted men is not according to the age groups or interest group to which they minister, but according to gift/vocation. These men are presented to the church in order to exercise certain God-given gifts. Logically, a spiritually gift is not primarily a particular age group ministry. There is no spiritual gift of working with young people or children. If there were, then there would be a gift of old people's work—a gift which few have claimed to have.

Children, young people, and young and older adults all need to benefit from the exercise of the continuing gifts of pastor, teacher, and evangelist.

Within the New Testament church, each gifted man performed the task related to his God-given ability. Thus, apostles, prophets, evangelists, and pastor-teachers cut across the sexes (Gal. 3:28), age groups (Acts 16:34), and interest groups (1 Tim. 6:17; Jas. 1:9-12) to perform their divinely sponsored tasks. This process of using the gifts of the Spirit is a vocational ministry rather than a sectional one.

It has always been implied that there is a lot in a name. In the case of the church staff worker, it is crucial. It is true, as some would repeatedly remind us, "No one competes with the pastor." The question is whether that means there can be only one person in a church exercising a pastoral function and gift. Administratively, it is true that there must be no competition with the senior pastor; however, the educational worker who ministers pastorally under the pastor-teach gift of Ephesians 4 should be recognized as doing so. Consequently, the term *education pastor* describes the ministry better than "Director of Christian Education." Church people often feel strange responding to a *director*, but find it easier to confide in a *pastor*. The *education pastor* is subject to the same call of God as the missionary, evangelist, or pastor.

Administrative Benefits of a Vocational Multiple Staff

It is extremely difficult to separate good administrative practice from biblical principle. The Bible admonishes us with reference to the gifts and in church worship to do all things decently and in good order (1 Cor. 14:40). A study of the vocational multiple staff ministry without a treatment of its administrative benefits would tell only part of the story. Both the staff and the church benefit greatly from such a staff relationship.

Benefits for the Members of the Pastoral Staff

Stronger Motivation

Probably the predominant administrative benefit of a vocational multiple staff is personal motivation. Business has taught that no amount of money can make a man productive and happy if he is not interested in what he is doing. If he is to be satisfied and perform his work well, a man must be motivated. Motivation is an extremely important factor in any multiple staff church ministry. Unless each man is highly motivated in the performance of his job responsibilities, friction and shoddy work will result. Only a truly vocational ministry can prevent this potential trouble. An examination of motivation reveals some reasons which are crucial.

A man has five basic needs in addition to the needs of the spiritual life. While these needs are not directly addressed in the Bible, observation seems to support their existence in reality. Abraham Maslow motivational needs chart identifies them as such:

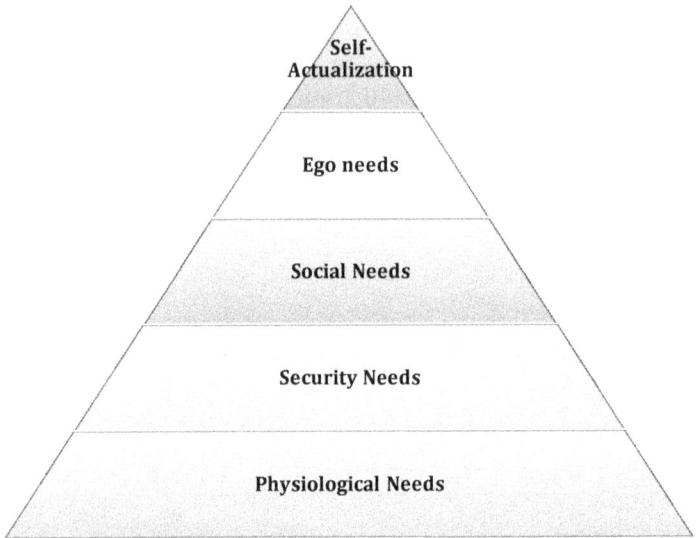

Self-Actualization

Ego needs

Social Needs

Security Needs

Physiological Needs

As was previously pointed out, there are two views of the multiple staff with distinctively different resultant ministries. The implications of these views become pronounced when examined in light of the five basic motivational needs of man. Some staff members find all five areas of need being starved or hampered in their church ministry. A subordinate man often finds his salary is inadequate to support his family. Almost invariably, it is significantly lower than his senior pastor's salary. Therefore, his *physiological* needs may not be met. The average tenure of an assistant pastor or youth pastor is often less than two years. The need for *security* is often violated. This may well account for the shortage of staff men over thirty-five years of age.

Where the people honor their senior pastor and fail to understand their relationship to other members of the staff, there is a definite problem of *social* need. The people may tend to invite the senior pastor out to events, give him gifts at Christmas, and write him thank you notes, while other staff members must find their own social affirmation.

Self-confidence and respect are hard to muster when one is the "second man" to whom few people go with big problems or needs. Youth pastors struggle with this when unable to minister to parents because they listen only to the senior pastor. Yet, if a man is to grow and expand his abilities and desires to work hard, his _ego_ needs must be met.

Finally, there is the problem of *self-actualization*. This is easily recognized as a most important need in any person's vocational life; yet for the "other man" on the church staff, it may be the most difficult to attain. As one pastor stated while comparing his position with that of the youth pastor, "I have sought the greater gift." The feeling that the other staff responsibilities of the church are of secondary importance promotes a feeling that, no matter how hard a staff member tries, he can never know the joy of fulfilling a high and holy call which before God is of equal importance with the senior pastor.

There are other benefits for men involved in a vocational multiple staff. They include *better personal relationships* with the staff, *an awareness of the call of God*, and a *sense of purpose or life goal.* They are discussed below in this order.

Improved Personal Relationships

Being a member of a vocational multiple staff in a church has parallels to being a member of football team. On a football team, there must be a quarterback who calls the signals. At the same time, there are other men on that team that are equally valuable. Each man has his specialty to perform. A quarterback without a tackle is just as useless as a tackle without a quarterback. Each must depend on the other and respect the other's ability.

In much the same way, the members of a vocational staff must be interdependent and respectful of the position and ability of each of the others. Overloading of individuals and restraint of the exercise of individual gifts are both kept at a minimum. Instead, a "team spirit" dominates for the glory of God.

An Awareness of the Call of God

In football, the quarterback brings in the signals and passes judgment on the options, yet there is an equality of function and importance. In fact, there are a number of quarterbacks who have been passed up in NFL drafts in favor of good linemen. This is a good picture of the vocational staff relationship. The senior pastor is called of God to be the church leader administratively. At the same time, God calls the education pastor or outreach pastor to fulfill his God-given ministry with equal importance. Each is called of God to work in harmony with the whole. Without this, the biblical pattern of God's call to the ministry gives way to the whims of each individual senior pastor.

A Sense of Purpose

An illustration of a clearer sense of purpose for the education pastor or associate might be found in a comparison of the positions of the football team. How many tackles are playing the tackle position in order to become quarterback someday? Yet on contemporary sectional multiple staffs, many men in the assistant or youth pastor position are learning pastoral responsibilities with the goal of one day becoming a senior pastor. Within the vocational multiple staff ministry, there is room for a man to be called of God as an education or outreach pastor for life. He does not have to consider his ministry as a step in "growing up."

In addition to these benefits are such things as a broader range of ministry, mutual sharing of program ideas, and combined spiritual strength. For mature men who have a grasp of God's call and know where they are going in life, the vocational multiple staff can provide an ideal working relationship.

Benefits for the Church

The vocational multiple staff benefits the church also. It would do well to consider some of these benefits briefly.

Unity of the People

A vocational division of ministry creates unity throughout the church program instead of fragmenting it. With a sectional ministry, the congregation is often split into loyalties because of the isolation of the ministries of the staff members. Group loyalties are built up when one of the staff is considered to be the leader of a fragment of the church. The adults tend to consider the preacher of God's Word to be "their pastor," while looking upon the assistant pastor or youth pastor as "pastoring our young people." At the same time, the youth give allegiance to this usually younger staff member. Because the ministry of the church has been divided by age, it becomes a situation in which two distrusting churches may actually exist in the same edifice.

Under a vocational multiple staff, people from all ages and interests unite in contributing to the program. When the education, outreach, or worship/music pastor attempts some new program in this situation, he finds acceptance and support for the program on a broad base. Without broad-based support, the associate pastor becomes quite powerless to lead a particular program of the total church. At the same time, the pastor may find that his sermons are being tuned out by the youth of the church. After all, if he spends all of his time with the adults, what is to persuade the youth that he is *really* interested in them as well? He tends to take his place on the other side of the "generation gap." It is a basic church axiom: where a man spends quality time, he will have support and a hearing. By ministering to the entire congregation, a unified vocational staff will produce a unified church. Divisive group loyalties will tend to disappear.

Coordination of the Program

The vocational multiple staff concept of organizing the church ministry functions with fewer conflicts. When two or more men work with the same group of people, each functioning area of his divine call and gifts, each must consider the desires and programs of the other staff members. As partners in God's program for a church, they unite to produce balanced events throughout the church year. At any given time, one member of the staff knows what is happening in the program of any age group. Goals, purposes, and calendar events can be easily correlated because each member of the staff ministers to all the people. The end result of this is that families are not in conflict because the education pastor plans a high school retreat on the same weekend the pastor plans a workshop for parents. If the church has a Christian school, it would aid coordination greatly for the education pastor to oversee the principal and that area of the church's ministry as well.

Multiple Pastoral Care

This means that both the three-year-old and the ninety-year-old of the church will have two or three pastors rather than one. The ninety-year-old receives the ministry of the Word in sermon and comfort from the senior pastor and receives training and ministry/counsel from the education pastor. The three-year-old is trained and guided under the direction of the education pastor, but sees much of the pastor in his house calls and visits to those ministering in the educational agencies of the church. Obviously, each member of the staff will spend more time in his specialty than in that of his associate, and this may mean that he spends more time with certain age groups at given periods of time. However, in case of emergency or crisis, any member of the staff can enter any home with rapport and self-confidence, taking with him the necessary comfort, advice or leadership.

The people of the church will be willing to accept the ministry of a vocational staff member because his ministry has been related to everyone in the church. They will not say, "Maybe we should call pastor so and so from the church across town. Our youth pastor can't handle these situations." Rather, they will say, "Our other pastor will be just fine since our senior pastor is out of town."

Implications for Present Practice

As in the case of most proposed changes in a leadership concept, there are already "normal" traditional ways of viewing the multiple staff. The vast majority of training schools, churches, pastors, and even potential "second men" are already familiar with the growing church adding an "assistant pastor" or "youth pastor" to aid the man who becomes the senior pastor. Both of these titles have historical merit as well as practical application today. However, neither "assistant pastor" nor "youth pastor" is any more biblical than "education pastor" or "associate pastor." The real question boils down to what makes the most sense, will fulfill biblical roles, and will meet the needs of the total ministry most effectively.

The Need for Completing Skills

Staff growth from one pastor to two or three pastors is an extremely important step for a church. The question "Whom shall we add first?" is always pertinent. It is my belief that a *Pastor of Christian Education* would seem to be the logical second position. The sheer number of laymen hours invested in education-related ministries would necessitate supervision.

An *Outreach Pastor* would join the team as the third pastor. The outreach pastor position is gaining interest in more recent church history. Normally, the result of his ministry is church growth. If the senior pastor has strength in the Christian education ministries, the church may want to call an outreach pastor as the first addition to the staff, even before a pastor Christian education or youth. He would normally be involved in organizing outreach ministries, training laymen in evangelism and discipling, and enfolding new members of all ages into the church.

A *Youth Pastor* would be added as the fourth staff member and normally work under the leadership of the Pastor of Christian Education along with eventual pastors of children's ministries and adult ministries. This type of youth pastor is highly trained to specialize in all facets of reaching, winning, training, and counseling the youth segment of the church, as well as their parents. Sometimes the youth pastorate is combined with music. Any of the other associates may be trained to lead the music ministry as well. For some churches, a pastor of worship/music may be added earlier and in a full-time capacity in a large church. Eventually, all large churches will probably need and seek full-time leadership of a worship/music ministry to all ages.

The key concept of concern here is that a team should be developed that has differing but complementing gifts and perspectives, so that the needs of the total congregation can be met. Two or three "clones" of the senior pastor will not bring this about. A team of complementing professionals can carry on a long-term ministry that brings harmony and growth to the church as well as challenge and biblical fellowship to the staff.

Two assumptions are very important to review at this point in the discussion. First, at any and all stages of a church's growth most pastoral leadership functions could be delegated to qualified godly laymen. However, lay-led ministries tend to plateau because of the sheer weight of administrative time required, and eventually this forces consideration of a full-time vocational pastor for the area of need. Second, before adding a second pastor, a qualified church secretary should be employed and custodial areas be covered as well. Otherwise, the church will have a pastoral team involved in a level of detail that may actually be poor stewardship of their time, training, and cost.

Assistant Pastors Only Assist

Why is it self-defeating to refer to any additional pastors as "assistant" pastors? When a church calls an assistant pastor, there are normally three underlying assumptions in place. First, the new man's job description will be very general and his purpose will be to engage in whatever ministries the senior pastor may deem necessary at the particular time. Consequently, the duties may change frequently and be closely tied to whatever project or emphasis is at hand.

Second, the assistant pastor is usually perceived as an extension of the senior pastor. The assistant pastor, in effect, also works on those things the senior pastor is promoting through his particular gifts or interests. Consequently, the congregation has in reality one "larger" pastor who can now get more accomplished through the extra body and mind of his assistant, rather than two pastors called of God to lead them in different strengths, areas, and gifts. The net result is having one and a half pastors rather than two full pastors.

The third frequently underlying assumption is that the assistant is in his position to learn and develop until such time as God will him to his own pastorate as a "senior pastor" or a one-man staff. The practical out-working is that assistant pastorates are short term and the best men will be gone the quickest. Consequently, the people learn to not build strong relationships with them and to not plan ministries or their lives around the assistant's work.

However, an assistant pastor can be a very helpful and significant staff person as he, the senior pastor, and the church enter into his assisting ministry fully aware of the assumptions and perceptions mentioned previously. An older pastor who comes to a staff to "assist" in a specific area of the church ministry can have a long and productive ministry.

SOME RECOMMENDATIONS

If the vocational multiple staff is to become a common procedure in churches, several considerations must be made by churches, colleges, seminaries, and other con-cerned agencies as well as by the men who are involved in multiple staff ministries.

The Associate Pastor Must Be Worthy of the Title

Too often the training and background of the educational worker or assistant keeps him from functioning
in a pastoral role. The education pastor must spend
time dealing with souls, winning and counseling them
for the Lord. The same standards of spiritual life (Tit.
1:6-9; 1 Tim. 3:1-7) and hard work must be followed
as for the senior pastor. Shoddy work and immaturity
do not cause the people to confide in a man, regardless
of his title.

**Pastor's Associations and Fellowships Must Include
Associate Pastors**

Instead of the pastors and educational or youth workers
always meeting separately, it would be good for them
to share and work together. Both callings need to get
to know each other instead of meeting separately,
which fosters distrust and misunderstanding. There is
a real need for harmony and acceptance between the
various callings of God.

**Associate Pastor Positions in the Local Church
Must Not Be Viewed as Temporary**

Hard feelings, confused lives, and wasted years have
resulted from the number of Christian education workers who see the educational or youth pastor position as
a stepping-stone to the pulpit. The associate pastor
must be able to see himself happy in a similar ministry

twenty years later. The stepping-stone concept only fosters distrust by senior pastors and degrades the position of the associate. Not all preachers are called to be senior pastor.

The Associate Pastor Must Experience a More Extensive Training Program

The training of the educational, outreach, worship/music, or youth pastor must be as great as that of the preaching pastor. Without a theologically comprehensive curriculum, coupled with field training, he goes "green" to minister in a large church. Only the large church is able to call a multiple staff. Preaching pastors often start with smaller churches and work up through their "errors," while the associate pastor finds himself expected to handle 500 people when fresh out of school. When he cannot handle the job, he becomes discouraged. This leads to a rejection of his profession, not only by himself, but by the senior pastor and people as well. Seminary and internship training may be essential to prevent early failure and disillusionment. Training in Christian school philosophy would aid him in churches that have Christian schools.

Church Multiple Staff Members Must Be Compatible

Most frustration and discouragement will be avoided when more emphasis is placed upon tests of compatibility in staff selection. It takes compatible personalities to have a consistently close and fruitful

relationship. There can be few secrets in a team ministry. Both men must know they can trust each other.
Bullheaded dictators make poor team members, as do
weak-kneed complainers. The associate pastors must
never undercut the senior pastor.

**Multiple Staff Members Must Sell the Vocational
Concept to the Congregation**

In order for the church to reap the benefits of a vocational multiple staff relationship, there must be a
conscious effort on the part of the staff members to sell
the concept. This calls for the senior pastor to be a
"big man" who is secure in the Lord. The senior pastor can make or break any efforts the associate pastor
may attempt, but he must be willing to share his position with another man who has equally valid call of
God. The following are some suggestions for selling
the team ministry to the church people.

1. The pastor may preach sermons on his relationship to the associate pastor and the people's
   relationship to him as well. He must point out
   the biblical basis of these relationships.
2. The pastor will be careful to use the title "Pastor So-and-so" whenever he refers to the
   associate pastor or other pastoral staff members. This shows the people that he has high
   regard for his partner and esteems him as a co-
   servant of Jesus Christ.
3. Warmth and a sense of rapport must prevail
   within the staff. This will draw them close together and bring the people's warmth to rest on

them as a team. The staff member must be careful to respect and encourage his senior pastor publicly and privately.

4. If the senior pastor sits on the platform in the worship services, the associates should as well. They should all take an active part as much as possible. Attendance at deacon board meetings is also essential.

5. The associate pastor must be seen on house calls, visitation, and hospital calls, as well as involved in evangelism if he is to be viewed as an equal member of the pastoral team.

If these things are practiced before the people, soon they will get the "big picture" and rejoice in the blessing of having two or more pastors. They will understand the spiritual and vocational equality. This is necessary in order for each man to have a truly productive ministry as he labors to serve the church to which God has called him.

Designing and developing a church pastoral staff is an extremely important exercise for senior pastors, deacons, and congregations. Without a well-prayed-over and thought-out philosophy, almost permanent patterns can be established that may affect the church negatively for generations.

Practical Application Exercises

1. Write a paragraph or two explaining why you agree or disagree—based on the information provided in the biblical references embodied in this chapter—that the vocational multiple staff model is best suited to adapt to the gifts of the pastoral staff and to the needs of each local church.

2. Interview five of your church's lay persons and two deacons. Ask them if they can relate better to a *director* or a *pastor*. Compare their answers to the information provided in this chapter and write a 1,000 word summation of your findings.

3. Visit a church that has an active pastoral staff and one with a single pastor. Compare the two organizational structures and identify why you believe one structure is beneficial to the one church and not the other.

Recommended Resources for Further Study

Crumroy, Otto F., Kukawka, Stan & Whitman, Frank, Church Administration and Finance Manual: Resources for Leading the Local Church. Church Publishing, Inc., 1998. (ISBN 978-0-819-21747-9)

Gilbert, Larry & Spear, Cindy, The Big Book of Job Descriptions for Ministry: Complete Descriptions of Nearly Every Ministry Job in the Church! Gospel Light Publications, 2002. (ISBN 978-0-830-72918-0)

Gilbert, Larry, Team Ministry: Gifted to Serve. ChurchGrowth.org, 2015. (ISBN 978-1-570-52333-5)

Pyle, William T., Experiencing Ministry Supervision: A Field-based Approach. Broadman & Holman, 1994. (ISBN 978-0-805-41163-8)

Spaite, Wil M., Selecting Effective Pastoral Staff: How to Find the Right Fit for Your Church. Beacon Hill Press, 2004. (ISBN 978-0-834-12101-0)

Westling, Harold J., Church Staff Handbook: How to Build an Effective Ministry Team. Kregal Academic, 1997. (ISBN 978-0-825-49425-3)

Deacon Ministry vs Deacon Board

One of the key components to the administration of the 21st Century Church is to properly identify the composition of Deacons. The very word *deacon* has been known to send shudders up some people's spines, not the least of which includes many pastors. As a practical exercise, compose a list of whatever comes to mind when you think of the word *deacon*. You may have possibly included responses like "godly," "controlling," "mean-spirited," "helpful," "compassionate," "negative," and more!

Hopefully, the words *servant* and/or *leader* were included as well. While the same kind of responses could describe how several people view *pastor*, this chapter examines various matters surrounding the nature and duties of deacons, in order to answer definitively what a deacon should be.

The high qualifications for the bishops (Pastors) and deacons found in 1 Timothy 2 clearly indicate that the New Testament Churches looked to these Church leaders for examples in Christian living. This continues to hold true even today. The Church, as Christ left it, had nothing but the preacher and the congregation; and the preacher was given the keys to the kingdom (Matt. 16:19) meaning the authority to appoint or to call any other lay persons, who had the spirit of Christ, to assist him with his administrative responsibilities.

The Origin of the Diaconate

If you were to ask the average deacon when the deacon ministry originated, he will refer to Acts 6. Much of the early 20th century literature supports this view. E. C. Dargan, an influential voice in Baptist ecclesiology, noted that although the word generally refers to servant, it came to be used of the officer. Although others prefer to challenge this assumption, the first lay persons which the apostles called were the chosen seven (Acts 6:3). Therefore, the deacon in the Baptist Church must not mistake this appointment by the apostles of old, and his appointment by his pastor with the approval of the church, as a divine ordination from God.

Board or Body (Management or Ministry)

The most contentious aspect of deacon ministry among Baptist churches is its function. Is a group of deacons a board or a body? Is their primary role that of management or ministry?

Several have sought to trace the role of the deacon throughout church history. The first few centuries reveal deacons expressing practical service, especially benevolence. The Middle Ages, however, shows the diaconate evolving into initial training for the priesthood. The Reformation Period recovered the emphasis of benevolent ministry to the poor. By the late-18th

century, however, deacons began concerning themselves with the secular business, primarily by manag-
managing the material and financial issues. It is the
belief of the Charleston Association that the deacon is
to relieve the minister from the secular concerns of the
church and their business is to serve tables. It is be-
lieved that this management mindset arose out of
secular problems, where business decisions were made
during a meal around a wooden (board) table.
"Boards" became known as any group that made decisions. This view eventually passed into the church
among deacons making deacon boards standard by the
19th century.

Most of the 20th century saw this trend continue as addressed by P.E. Burroughs in 1929. The deacon is
entrusted with the care of the material interests of the
church. He is to care for the properties of the church,
its building, pastor's home, and material holdings. He
is to direct and safeguard the financial side of its ministry while serving in the materiality of the church.
Deacons, by virtue of their office, must share with the
pastor this responsibility of leadership which really
amounts to authority and rule. At the same time it
should go without saying that deacons are not be ruling
elders or managing directors seeing that the church is
viewed as pure democracy.

Issues that signal when deacons function as church
business managers include

(1) When the deacons' responsibilities are composed solely of business management matters.

(2) When deacons administer the affairs of the church primarily as a business operation.

(3) When deacons are viewed as the decision makers in most business affairs.

(4) When business efficiency seems to predominate the activities of deacons.

The Scriptures do no not list specific duties which deacons are to perform. However, the Bible does focus on deacon qualifications. Deacons who measure up to the biblical qualifications are equipped to minister to the spiritual needs of the people. Thus, because they are spiritually qualified, deacons should help carry out the pastoral ministry areas of the church. Pastoral ministries is a large umbrella that includes caring for church members and people in the community through a Deacon Family Ministry Plan, counseling, preaching/witnessing, providing benevolence, maintaining fellowship in the church, and helping the church achieve its mission.

Pastoral ministry is not the only area where deacons can benefit the church. The ministry options are virtually endless, including serving as greeters and ushers, helping in worship, administering the Lord's Supper, and serving on committees (finance, personnel, property, and more). While deacons may serve in finances and material aspects, it is the belief of this author that they are not mandated to be the only, or even primary, financial/material decision-makers in the church.

Historically, many Baptist churches in the 19th and 20th centuries were small and rural with part-time preachers. Deacons stepped up to the plate to take care of the church property and eventually made decisions on other church matters. The 20th century has witnessed Baptist growth in other settings, especially cities and metropolitan areas. These settings tend to keep pastors longer and do not expect deacons to make most of the church's decisions. Thus, recent decades have argued against deacon management (decision-making board) philosophy of the previous two centuries while underscoring a deacon ministry (service-oriented body) philosophy. Many older churches, typically in small towns and rural communities, still function with deacon boards in place while new churches, especially in larger cities, emphasize a deacon ministry that serves.

Deacons Relating to Pastors

All-to-often a pastorate has come to an end because at least one deacon butted heads with the pastor. There are times, to be sure, that the pastors bear some, or most, of the responsibility in poor relationships to deacons. Because this chapter's focus is deacons, however, a few suggestions follow to enhance the ways deacons relate to pastors.

Deacons who recognize and appreciate that the pastor's business is the highest of all can maximize the pastor's time by meeting with him, when necessary, so that valuable time is not spent in his travel to and from a deacon's home or place of business. Moreover, deacons serve the pastor well when they ensure that he receives a fair and reasonable compensation from the church. Helping bear the pulpit ministry, especially on

Sunday or Wednesday evenings, when the pastor needs to be away, also ministers to both the church and pastor, who does not have to go to great lengths to secure a replacement. Finally, regular prayer for the pastor and clear communication indicate support and cooperation in serving together to accomplish the church's mission. Deacons who pursue good relations with their pastors, especially in these areas, usually find enjoyment and fulfillment in serving the church together.

Sharing Ministry with the Pastor

The New Testament model of service and today's need point to deacons serving alongside the pastor in pastoral ministries as stated previously. Ernest E. Mosley speaks of caring, proclaiming, and leading as the interlocking and mutually supportive pastoral ministry responsibilities.

The three basic pastoral ministries tasks are:
1. To proclaim the Gospel to believers and unbelievers.
2. To care for the church's members and other persons in the community.
3. To lead the church in the achievement of its mission.

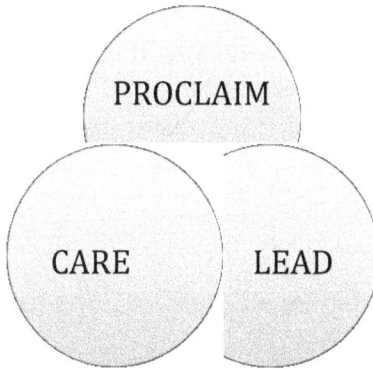

The pastor has the responsibility to lead the pastoral ministries team in carrying out these tasks. Mosley stated "As team leader, the pastor is responsible for equipping deacons for their ministry and drawing on all the resources available to them for training in order that they may be able to minister with increasing effectiveness. He will guide the deacons in discovering their responsibilities."

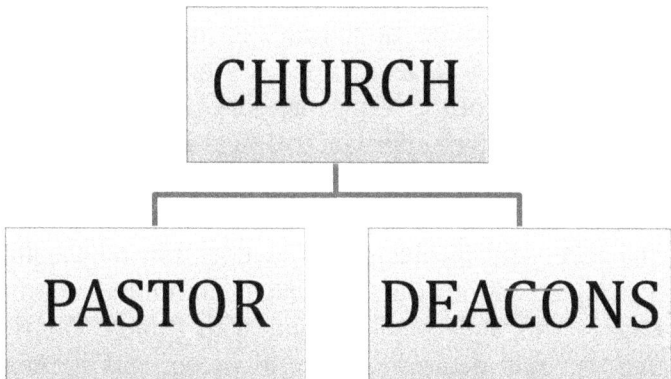

As partners with the pastor, deacons have the privilege and opportunity to share with him in modeling ministry to service. It is important to note that any disadisagreement between the pastor and deacon should be kept from the church in order for the church to function properly.

A High Pedigree – Qualifications for Deacons

Nearly every volume on deacons covers the important qualifications outlined in Scripture. Those who believe Acts 6 describes deacons attribute matters like being full of the Spirit, wisdom, and faith to their qualifications. Everyone agrees on the moral, doctrinal, and familial prerequisites in 1 Timothy 3, except when it comes to one issue: "the husband of one wife."

Some favor a "one wife at a time" kind of deacon; if the deacon is married at all using the interpretation that Paul is speaking against polygamy. Some promote only one living wife at a time, if married, and even caution against deacons' wives from denominations other than Baptist. Some authors contend that Paul gives his stamp of approval to Jesus' absolute rejection of divorce. While yet and still some remain more neutral on the issue, proclaiming that the sanctity of the marriage vow forbids adultery, does not allow plural marriages, and encourages sexual faithfulness in marriage. This author will concur with Robert Sheffield that the final decision single, divorced, and/or remarried deacons is to be left in the hands of the local church, preferably decided without personalities involved and with much prayer.

Most churches have some age requirement for deacons. The intent is that deacons should have broad enough adult experience to be able to minister maturely to a cross section of members. Of course, such maturity does not come to all persons at the same age. However, churches have most often set the minimum age at twenty-one or twenty-five.

Many churches also require prospective deacons to be church members for a specified period of time. This gives church members a more adequate opportunity to become familiar with their qualifications for deacon service. This time also gives prospective deacons an opportunity to become familiar with nature and style of the church and how deacons minister in it. A one-year requirement is most common, but some churches require as little as six months while others as much as two years.

Churches often require some external signs of commitment to the church. Most frequently cited is regular participation in church programs such as Sunday School, Church Training, Sunday worship services, and midweek prayer service. Deacons are often also expected to be tithers, giving 10 percent or more of their income through the church budget. A church may also require regular deacons' meeting attendance and participation in specific training for deacon ministry.

Other requirements usually drive from the biblical qualifications found in Acts 6:3 and 1 Timothy 3:8-13.

Duck. . . Duck. . . Deacon --- Electing Deacons

When it comes time to elect deacons, churches employ a variety of ways. A few practice open nomination from the floor, some accept nomination by a committee, too many allow the deacons to name their newcomers, a small number allow the pastor to nominate them, and all others call for a precise number of names to be written on a ballot.

No one system is fool-proof, but the written method seems to be the most practical. The church determines how many deacons are needed and the moderator instructs members during business how many names of qualified men should be written down (or checked off on a provided list). This practice saves those men with little or no votes from the embarrassment that could come from an open nomination. With every voting member of the church stating their preference, deacons, nominating committees, and pastors have less control over this facet of the church's life. No matter what method churches use, they are wise to state deacon qualifications clearly and screen/interview potential candidates in advance to determine if any questionable areas might exclude the man from deacon-service.

Serving 'til the Cows Come Home? --- Tenure

Just as differences of opinion exist over electing deacons, so it goes with their tenure.   Some Baptists
believe, "Once a deacon, always a deacon." This view
finds little support among the influential writers and
thinkers of the 20th century.   In fact, Burroughs cites
five reasons to jettison lifetime service. First, a deacon
may leave the church and go elsewhere.   His new
church is under no obligation to allow him to serve as a
deacon.   Second, a deacon may request to step down
from service due to a number of circumstances. Third,
a deacon's old age and limited activity may prevent
him from serving, at least in an active role. Fourth, the
church may ask the deacon to step down due to immo-
rality, doctrinal heresy, or a hindering attitude.
Finally, the church may have a rotation system in place
where every deacon ceases to serve for one or more
years after a period of active service (usually three to
five years).

Many churches now follow the rotation system. There
are certain merits to this method of service, for it

1. Provides a broader base of leadership, enabling
   more qualified persons to serve their church as
   deacons.
2. Provides a way for deacons who no longer
   want to serve to retire with grace.
3. Provides a way for deacons to renew themselves spiritually for greater ministry
   effectiveness.

4. Provides for a continually effective Deacon Family Ministry Plan.
5. Provides the church the opportunity to replace those deacons who, because of age, infirmity, or loss of interest, have become inactive and ineffective.
6. Provides the church with safeguards against the "board of directors" mentality among deacons.

Though a few disadvantages exist with rotation, the most obvious being that an extremely good deacon has to sit out for a period, the advantages clearly outweigh the disadvantages.

Some churches confer the title of "deacon emeritus" in recognition and honor for long-standing deacon service. The term emeritus means that the deacon has retired from an active position, usually when no longer physically able to carry out the duties of an active deacon. Some churches use other titles such as "life deacon" or "deacon for life."

Odds and Ends---Ordaining, Organizing, Training, and Soul-Winning

While chapters could be written on each of these areas, a common consensus exists about what each area is. Deacon ordination is a planned service, usually accompanied by the laying on of hands by either those already ordained or the whole church, whereby the church officially sets the new deacon apart for service. The preaching, singing, and praying should aim to honor the Lord while recognizing His involvement in the deacon's life. Even though ordinations do not impart any special power, the service should be meaning-meaningful to the deacon, his family, and the church.

On a different note, the deacon body which functions best is the one where organization is in place. A chairman and a secretary are necessities, for planning and recording deacon meetings and service. Depending on the size of the deacon body, a vice chair may be necessary. A few more organizational levels may be needed for larger churches to be more effective. Clearly written expectations of each officer and deacon bring a sense of purpose and mission to each deacon as he relates to his fellow deacons and to the church. Where a Deacon Family Ministry Plan is in place, eight to fifteen families fall under each deacon's care for one year. Each year the families are disbursed anew so that deacons get to know more people and so that families that may have been neglected receive the care they need.

Providing training for deacons, at least annually, enhances their effectiveness for ministry. Training may come from individual study books recommended by the pastor or deacon body, or seminars may be offered by the church, association, state, or a national conference/retreat. The purpose of such training is to help each deacon grow in the faith and his walk with the Lord, as well as his role among fellow deacons within the church.

Ultimately, the best deacon is a soul-winning deacon. The best service of the deacon, his highest function, is winning men to Christ. The most obvious expectation of deacons is in the proclamation of the gospel through preaching or witnessing, for every volume on the diaconate covers this subject. Thus, the best way a deacon can serve the church is through serving the lost by sharing the good news.

The Deacon Chairman

Although, it is my personal opinion that the Pastor serves as the Chairman of the Deacon body, I realize that it is common practice for such office to be filled by a vote of the deacons. The chairman of deacons is more than a presiding officer. The deacon chairman is one of the most important places of leadership in the church. According to Charles F. Treadway, the chairman is "a spiritual leader who has been given the opportunity of leading the deacons to fulfill their mission in the total area of deacon ministry."

The position provides a unique opportunity to work closely with the pastor. The two can build a special relationship of appreciation, encouragement, and support. The chairman's leadership style should be consistent with Jesus' instructions to his disciples in Mark 10:42-44.

The duties for the deacon chairman could include:

1. Lead the deacons in planning, conducting, and evaluating all of their work.
2. Plan, conduct, and evaluate deacons' meetings.
3. Provide deacons with adequate training and resources for their work.
4. Guide deacons in organizing and conducting a ministry to families in the church.
5. Serve as a member of the church council. Interpret deacon work to the council, and provide deacons with information about the total work of the church.
6. Report regularly to the church on the work of the deacons.
7. Give guidance to the pastoral ministries of the church when it is without a pastor.

Conclusion---Is a Deacon a Servant or a Leader?

Every book on deacons underscores that deaconship is distinctly a call to serve. Men are to be elected to the office of deacon with a view to service. In addition to service, however, each volume highlights the leadership office of deacons. Discouraged in recent decades from being the leaders of the church through a board of directors, deacons should be a part of the larger leadership team. They are leaders in their churches. Church members look to their deacons for leadership. The Bible depicts deacons as significant leadership figures in the New Testament church. In the end, deacons are servant-leaders, carrying out ministry to the congregation while helping lead the church to fulfill its mission.

Practical Application Exercises

1. In the beginning of this chapter, you were told if you asked a group of Baptists to list whatever comes to mind when they hear the word *deacon* that there would be many different responses. Now compose a list of what comes to your mind when you hear the word *Christian.* Interview a group of people—regardless of denomination—and ask them to make a list of whatever comes to mind when they hear the word *Christian.* Compare these lists with your list. Write a 3 paragraph summation.

2. Does your church have a Deacon Family Ministry Plan? If so, how has this plan benefit the church membership? If not, draft a plan and identify the potential benefits.

3. Do you believe that deacons should be married or can he be single? Explain with biblical references and other resources.

Recommended Resources for Further Study

Anyabwile, Thabiti M., Finding Faithful Elders and Deacons. Crossway, 2012. (ISBN 978-1-433-52995-5)

Bailey, Keith M., Servants in Charge: A Training Guide for Elders and Deacons. Moody Publishers, 2007. (ISBN 978-1-600-66974-3)

Herbster, Carl & Howerton, Kenneth, Pastors & Deacons: Servants Working Together. Ambassador International, 2010. (ISBN 978-1-935-50732-1)

Merkle, Benjamin L., 40 Questions about Elders and Deacons. Kregel Academic, 2008. (ISBN 978-0-825-49332-4)

Church Council & Standing Committees

The Church Council provides for the church member-ship to have a majority voice in the operational affairs of the Church with implementation and support being handled by the church staff. The Council also provides for a more unified, cohesive, and knowledgeable dis-cussion and decision-making of the issues affecting the church with a single body instead of the various dis-parate committees. Generally, each member on the council will serve on one of three committees; Person-nel Committee, Finance Committee or Membership Committee.

It is the primary task of the Church Council to help en-sure the church's mission and vision statements are accomplished. It is the Church Council's primary re-sponsibility to plan, promote, coordinate and evaluate the various programs, ministries of the church and to develop and maintain the church calendar.

The Church Council is generally comprised of the church ministerial staff, the deacon chairman, the Sun-day School superintendent, choir president, youth director and church librarian. Also, the chairpersons of all standing committees serve as members on the council as well. The pastor and deacons serve as ex-officio members of the council with voice and vote while the Church Secretary serves with voice only and no vote. Periodically, any and all other church leaders involved in the planning, scheduling and promotion of church activities, events and emphases are included temporarily as members of this Council.

The Church Council meets monthly for regular meetings and may be scheduled for special meetings by the Pastor at times determined necessary and appropriate by him. In addition to its regular monthly meetings, the Council meets annually in the final quarter of each year for the purpose of discussing/determining/developing means of implementing strategic plans for the upcoming year, which also includes the submission of projected budget needs to the Finance Committee for their consideration and inclusion in the church budget.

The Council is responsible for developing and coordinating a calendar of all programs, activities, emphasis, ministries and mission endeavors of the church and for presenting this calendar at monthly business meetings or the church's consideration and approval.

The Council is also responsible for facilitating the development of a statement of the mission and vision of the church, as well as the annual goals and objectives by which this mission and vision may be accomplished.

The Council is also responsible for communicating effectively and regularly with the church family and the community regarding all church programs, emphasis, ministries and missions endeavors, so that the church and community will be kept informed of what is happening at the church.

The Council also evaluates (both at monthly meetings and in the annual planning sessions) all aspects of church life and ministries and makes recommendations of ideas and plans that will foster and enhance the quality and variety of what the church offers to its membership and community.

The Council meets in special sessions sometime during the final quarter of the each year for the purpose of discussion, planning and identifying means of implementing strategic plans for the coming year and for sharing projected budget needs for the coming year which are to be submitted to the Finance Committee for consideration and inclusion in the annual church budget presented to the church.

The Council is to create and foster an environment among church leaders which facilitates cooperation and mutual support in all aspects of church life.

Members of the Church Council should make every effort to attend each meeting of the Council, making arrangements for a proxy when they cannot attend themselves.

Members of the Church Council are also expected to assist the pastor by equipping and maturing the church body. Members achieve this by participating in and encouraging the following:

- Regular Sunday School attendance
- Regular worship attendance

- Financial stewardship
- Partnering amongst all ministries
- Personal spiritual growth and commitment
- Promoting cross ministry interaction and support
- Attempting to resolve matters that may result in conflicts of varying degrees

It is ideal for council members to be rotated as well. For example, at the end of each service year six members will rotate off the council. Six new members will be elected to the council each year to serve 3-year terms.

Church Personnel Committee

The Personnel Committee should be composed of members elected annually upon the recommendation of the Committee on Committees or the Church body. If possible, this committee should include some church members who have experience in personnel matters in their secular employment. Any member of the Personnel Committee who has a member of their immediate family (spouse, child, sibling, or anyone living in their home) that is employed by the church in any capacity, should abstain from discussion and/or voting on any issues related to their employment. Members of the Personnel Committee should notify the committee immediately if any applicant is related so that no conflict of interest will take place in the discussion regarding hiring, dismissal, or benefits for that individual.

The Personnel Committee is responsible for personnel management for the church. These responsibilities will include the following:

A. Evaluate positions and recommend additions/deletions of positions putting these recommendations before the church for their approval.

B. Review, update and develop job descriptions for positions needed and approved by the church.

C. Work with the Church Finance and Budget Committee to determine possible compensation for positions approved by the church.

D. Receive resumes from persons seeking positions with the church, with the exception of the office of pastor or any other ministerial staff positions that the church has charged specific committees with the responsibility for filling the position.

E. Work closely with the Pastor Search Committee and the Church Finance Committee to develop a package for prospective pastoral candidates and other staff positions.

F. Interview and recommend qualified candidates for approved positions on the church staff as authorized.

G. Establish policies to assist the church to make the ministry and work of the church staff and employees effective and meaningful.

H. Policies should include, but are not limited to the following: Compensation, Workplace Guidelines, Benefits and Performance Standards.

The Personnel Committee should also provide to the congregation information and updates regarding personnel issues only as essential for the church to make a final decision regarding the hiring or dismissal of personnel. Confidentiality should be maintained at all times through this process.

The Personnel Committee works with the employees of the church to determine pay periods, the method to be used to record hours worked, overtime issues and payroll deductions. This committee also recommends to the church any policies related to personal appearance or dress code, office hours, attendance at staff meetings, tardiness or lateness, sexual or other forms of harassment, personal or romantic relationships, addictive behavior, outside employment and activities, use of church equipment, personal and ethical responsibilities, financial integrity, counseling sessions, confidentiality of church information, email usage, workplace safety and security.

The Personnel Committee also recommends for church approval policies related to but not limited to vacation, holidays and sick days. This committee collaborates with the Budget and Finance Committee on policies related to retirement participation, Social Security compensation as appropriate and health care insurance and reimbursements as appropriate.

It is the Personnel Committee who recommends for church approval performance standards which are specific, measurable, attainable, realistic, and trackable. Position descriptions should be used to determine the effectiveness of the employee or staff member in relation to their work. The committee will develop a performance evaluation process to be approved by the church and used annually. This committee will work with the Senior Pastor to set a time for performance evaluations. The committee may meet with the pastor to complete the evaluation or may request another individual or group within the congregation to evaluate the Pastor's work.

The Personnel Committee should meet on a monthly basis with the Chair calling special meetings as needed to deal with employee or staff concerns. The Chair should develop an agenda for each meeting and the committee should follow the agenda. Urgent or emergency items should be dealt with in a called meeting as necessary. No action should be taken or recommendations made without a quorum present and voting. The committee should report to the church on a regular basis to keep the church informed of issues as relating to personnel.

Finance Committee

The purpose of the Finance Committee is to oversee the finances and stewardship of the church in accordance with the mission of the church. The members are usually appointed by the Pastor with approval of the church body for 3-year terms. This committee should reflect specific expertise related to finances or business and should have been a member of the church for at least three years. Unlike any other committee in the church, the Pastor generally appoints the chair and vice-chair of the Finance Committee. A member of the committee is designated to take minutes at all committee meetings with a copy of such minutes archived in accordance with established church policy. The Pastor and a member of the staff designated by the pastor serve as non-voting, ex-officio members of the Finance Committee. This committee should meet at least on a monthly basis and are generally accountable to the Church Council and Deacons.

The duties of the Finance Committee include the following:

1. To serve as spiritual overseers of the financial affairs and stewardship of the church in accordance with the mission of the church.

2. To secure budget requests from the Ministerial Staff and church committees and teams in order to prepare a church budget. The Finance Committee should contact these entities by August 1, and the budget requests should be

returned to the Finance Committee by September 1.

3.   To prepare an annual budget that is aligned with the mission of the church and recommends that budget to the church for vote. The proposed budget should first be reviewed by the Church Council and the deacons at their October meetings before being presented to the church at the last business meeting of the fiscal year.

4.   To coordinate the annual church stewardship promotion with the Pastor and Ministerial Staff, Deacons, Sunday School superintendent, and other appropriate committees and teams. The planning of this stewardship promotion should begin no later than September 1.

5.   To insure the preparation of and to review the monthly church financial statement.

6.   To provide the financial statement at the monthly meetings of the Church Council and the Board of Deacons and at the quarterly church business meetings. This financial statement should include the following:
     a.   Year-to-date actual receipts and expenditures verses the current budget
     b.   The balance sheet
     c.   An investment summary

7. To review all receipts and expenditures monthly to assure compliance with the budget.

8. To review requests for budget revisions and requests for expenditures not in the current budget. Any request approved by the Finance Committee which cannot be funded by an annual contingency fund must be reviewed by the Church Council and the Deacons before being presented to the church for vote.

9. To establish and periodically review policies and procedures for financial controls.

10. To supervise the accounting system and recommend updates and changes as needed.

11. To supervise the financial operations of the church to ensure proper and timely counting and depositing of all church funds.

12. To supervise the proper and timely disbursement of all church funds.

13. To formulate and review policies and procedures relating to the Church Treasurers, including the disbursement of funds.

14. To periodically assess the need for a financial review or audit.

15. To establish and periodically review policies and procedures for designated gifts and funds.

16. To establish and periodically review policies and procedures for church investments.

17. To review investment allocation and performance.

18. To communicate and coordinate with the Risk Management and By-Laws Committee concerning risk management issues of a financial nature.

19. To develop and maintain documented operating procedures for this team and to furnish copies to the Church Council, Deacons and Pastor.

20. To provide a copy of this team's operating procedures and PDO to each new committee member to better train and equip new members.

Practical Application Exercises

1. Interview three ministers who are currently serving in churches.
   a. Write down this information from each interview:
      i. Does the church have a Church Council in place? Why or why not?
      ii. How many standing committees does the church have?
      iii. Aside from the three committees identified in this chapter, name another that is utilized by your church and its principle function to the church.

2. Research church committees in various denominations. How many appear in more than one denomination? What are the differences of its composition or primary function? Write a 2-page essay proclaiming your findings.

3. Write a paragraph detailing the importance of the standing committees in relation to church administration.

Recommended Resources for Further Study

Bisagno, John R., Pastor's Handbook. B&H Publishing Group, 2001. (ISBN 978-1-433-67389-4)

Cothen, Th.D., Joe H., Equipped for Good Work: A Guide for Pastors. Pelican Publishing, 2002. (ISBN 978-1-455-60385-5)

Eason, Steven P., Making Disciples, Making Leaders: A Manual for Developing Church Officers. Geneva Press, 2004. (ISBN 978-1-611-64439-5)

George, Denise, What Pastors Wish Church Members Knew: Helping People Understand and Appreciate Their Leaders. Zondervan, 2009. (ISBN 978-0-310-57483-5)

Melander, Rochelle & Eppley, Harold, Growing Together: Spiritual Exercises for Church Committees. Augsburg Fortress Publishers, 1998. (ISBN 978-0-806-63716-7)

Walden, Ken J., Practical Theology for Church Diversity: A Guide for Clergy and Congregations. Wipf and Stock Publishers, 2015. (ISBN 978-1-498-26998-8)

Woods, Benny, My Wounded Heart: Responding Positively to Hurt in Order to Return to Wholeness. WestBow Press, 2015. (ISBN 978-1-512-711332-2)

The Nuts & Bolts of the Church

Fulfilling a church's mission requires taking the time to develop a strategy, planning the steps to get it done and management of the process. Managing the process requires identifying who needs to do what, by when and holding them accountable for what they are responsible for doing.

A strategic plan is only as effective as the goals that are written to implement it. And, goals are only as effective as the people who are responsible for completing them. It is leadership's responsibility to make sure it gets done. In this chapter, we will identify seven steps to implementing church strategy.

1. Vision, Mission and Values

The first step is to writing a church vision, mission and values statement. This step is important because it helps with understanding the why the ministry exists (mission) and what it is trying to accomplish (vision).

It also clarifies the guiding principles (values) by which it operates and makes decisions. This is arguably the most important step because it sets the direction for the church. Without clarity of vision, any organization is susceptible to steering off course.

A vision statement provides direction and a target for the church. It is a tool to help the organization fulfill what God has called it to do. It is the bullseye! The value of a church vision statement is that it gives church leadership, employees and congregants a shared goal. Every organization needs to understand where it is going before it can develop a strategic plan and map out steps for how to get there.

A church vision statement is typically two to three sentences that describe what the church hopes to become or achieve. Some organizations write paragraphs describing their vision, but the shorter the statement, the more likely employees, volunteers and members will be able to absorb it, memorize it, and explain it to others.

It is important for the entire congregation to have a good understanding of what the church is trying to accomplish so that everyone can buy into and support the vision.

Writing the church's vision, mission and values statement should be an exercise that is done by the church board and some senior church members or staff. It is never done by a single individual. Ideally, this would be done in a retreat setting, such as a private room in a restaurant, a hotel conference room, or someone's home. It just needs to be a place without interruptions and distractions.

The beauty of the church is that God blesses churches with members who have a wide variety of gifts, and a church congregation may have professionals available who are gifted at facilitation and may be interested in facilitating a vision, mission and values session. If there is no one on board or in the congregation who has this skill set, it may be worth investing in a couple of hours with a professional who can help. Regardless, the facilitator should drive the process and not the vision. An experienced facilitator will know how to do this.

A visioning session is the "writing-on-tablet" process and should be prayed through before the session begins. The goal is to articulate God's will for the church. Depending on the number of people in the session, have the group break down into units of 3-4 people, provide each group with a flip chart, and have them discuss and answer the following questions:

- Who are we?
- Where does God want to use us to do?
- What do we want this church look like?
- Where do we want to be 1, 5, 10 years from now?
- As a group, create a newspaper headline about something the church has done/accomplished at some future point. This helps the group visualize the future.

Combine ideas, and at the end of this session:

- Have all the units come back together and tell the group the thoughts and ideas they came up with.

- Use the entire group to pick the best and most consistent thoughts and ideas from each of the smaller groups and simply write common words on a flipchart.
- Go around the room and allow all the participants to begin to add/subtract and formalize the sentence structure of the statement. Have a laptop available to use a thesaurus, dictionary and encyclopedia/search engine as references.

Once a couple of sentences have been written, read them out loud to the group again and determine if the entire group agrees that the statement reflects a common direction and describes a picture of an ideal future state of the church. Following are some example vision statements:

Caterpillar: Be the global leader in customer value.

DuPont: The vision of DuPont is to be the world's most dynamic science company, creating sustainable solutions essential to a better, safer and healthier life for people everywhere.

Heinz: Our Vision, quite simply is to be the world's premier food company, offering nutritious, superior tasting foods to people everywhere.

Sears: To be the preferred and most trusted resource for the products and services that enhance home and family life.

Avon: To be the company that best understands and satisfies the product, service and self-fulfillment needs of women globally.

Once the vision statement is written, do a similar exercise to come up with a mission statement. Remember a mission statement is a short description of why the organization exists. Vision and mission statements are the cornerstone for decision-making.

While in the same units, spend 20-30 minutes writing down descriptive words for why the church exists. After all the units have written their ideas on the flip chart, have each unit present its ideas to the whole group. Using one flip chart, combine ideas and begin wordsmithing the ideas until the group creates a short phrase that reflects all ideas. Have all the units to read the final statements and come to an agreement that the phrase truly reflects the mission of the church and why it exists.

Once there is a vision and mission statement, break the group into units again and allow them 20 minutes or so to list values (value = a principle, standard, or quality considered worthwhile or desirable) of the organization. Remember, these will become shared values or principles that the organization operates by.

Once each unit has its list, have them present it to the entire group. Combine ideas and refine them into one list. There are usually a lot of ideas that overlap (which is a good thing). Ideally, a list of values should be 5-10 words. The goal is for people who align themselves with the organization to be able to simply memorize the vision, mission and values. The more concise the better.

Once the vision, mission and values statement is finalized, think through a communication plan to share it with members, volunteers and employees. Invest in some frames and display the statement in visible areas of the building, on the church website and other printed materials.

That wasn't so difficult, was it? Many churches and nonprofit organizations fail to come up with a vision, mission and values statement because the process scares them, but with the right people in the room, it can be done in a few hours. Once a Vision, Mission and Values statement is written, the strategic planning process can begin!

2. Strategic Plan

After the vision, mission and values are written, a church strategic plan can be developed. The plan simply maps out the necessary steps to achieve the ministry's mission and vision. This kind of plan can be both short term (3-6 months) and long term (1-3 years). There was a time when strategic plans went as far out as five or ten years, but because of rapidly changing conditions, shorter term plans seem to be more common.

The first step is to identify the outcome – what it is you want to accomplish in three years. Take some time to brainstorm or visualize what that future state looks like. This will be the beginning of the plan. For example, strategic objectives or outcomes may be things like building a Bible school, planting churches, sending missionaries to certain parts of the world or developing worship leaders – whatever supports the church vision.

Next create a timeline for completion of objectives and determine how many weeks, months or years it will realistically take to complete the objectives. This is done by thinking through the high-level action steps needed to complete the tasks involved.

Strategic Objectives	Timeline		
	Year 1	Year 2	Year 3
Reduce operating budget by 5%, from $1M to $950,000.			
Grow volunteer base by 20%, from 250 to 350.			
Increase church membership from 1200 to 1500.			
Plant new church 50 miles from current location.			

Once you've identified what it is you want to accomplish (this should line up with the mission/vision) the next step is to start mapping out what it will take to get there. For example, to plant a church, you need to ask the question, what the steps that need to be taken? – i.e.: identify church plant leader, identify new church location, decide on church model, transition plan for leader, timeline to new church opening, etc.

This detailed planning can be put in the format of an action plan. An action plan is merely a written document outlining the objectives (goals), action steps, responsible person(s), possible team members, due date for each action step and implementation status.

Mapping this out creates a visual that is easy to see at a glance for what needs to be done, by whom and by when.

Objective	Action Step	Responsible Person(s)	Due Date
Plant church 50 miles from current church location	Identify Church plant leader	Church Board	June 15, 20XX Year 1
	Identify new church location	Church Board	December 31, 20XX – Year 2
	Decide on church model	Church Board	September 30, 20XX – Year 2
	Create transition for new church leader	Church Board/ Senior leaders	June 30, 20XX – Year 2
	Timeline for new church opening	Senior Leadership	December 31, 20XX – Year 1
	Open new church	Senior Leadership	September, 20XX – year 3

As you create the action plan document, you will identify objectives or steps that individual church departments need to take to support this strategic objective. And, as each department identifies their goals and objectives, it provides the information needed to write individual (or volunteer) job descriptions and goals, which support departmental goals, which support organizational goals and ultimately the strategic plan.

When goals and objectives are written to have a straight line influence on the strategic plan it helps to achieve the long-term goals of the organization.

3. Organizational Goals

Goals are important because they provide direction, clarify job roles, give something to strive for, show how far you've come and help make the vision attainable. Having goals written down makes it more real and achievable. It allows you to see where you are going and the steps to get there.

Church goals should be written at the organizational level as the first step in strategic implementation. This involves high level goals that the church as a whole is trying to accomplish. These high level goals are typically what a Business Administrator is accountable for to the board or governing body.

As the organization works toward accomplishing the strategic plan there needs to be a structured process to take the organization from where it is to where it wants to be. This can be done by developing annual organizational goals that are written to break the long-term goals into bite-sized pieces.

This step also provides the framework to accomplish them in steps and stages, rather than the overwhelming task of trying to do them all at once, and a tool to monitor its progress. This is done by spreading the responsibility of the goals to the departmental and staff level. This step helps to ensure that what staff is doing day-to-day, lines up with the vision and goals of the organization, and keeps employees focused on church priorities.

The structured process should include a cycle that begins with writing goals, communicating expectations, monitoring performance toward goals, assessing performance and lastly ends with the performance appraisal.

This cycle is repeated annually. Once the organization has some direction for what it wants to accomplish during the next twelve months, the priorities can be shared at the department level. This step ensures that there is a person or group of people with responsibility for completing those goals.

Example Year 1 Annual Church Goals

- Increase weekly attendance by 10% (120 people based on 1200 member church). This supports the strategic objective of growing the church to 1500 people in three years.
- Increase the number of church volunteers by 20% (50 new volunteers based on 250 current volunteers). This supports the strategic objective of growing the volunteer base by 20%, from 250 – 350 volunteers.

- Decrease operating expenses by 5%. This supports the strategic objective of reducing operating expenses by 5%.

4. Departmental Goals

Once there is defined church goals, goals should then be delegated to the respective ministry heads or department managers. This is where the chain-of-command or organizational structure delegates responsibilities for completing goals. For example, a Business administrator may have responsibility to achieve goals at the organizational level but may use the help of a ministry head or volunteer to accomplish those goals.

The ministry head or volunteer may then use employees or volunteers to help achieve goals. Now you take these Church (organizational) annual goals and break them down at the department level. This requires assigning the goal to a specific department. For example, the church goal of increasing weekly attendance by 10% can be delegated to several different departments but one specific department might be adult education.

Objective (goal)	Action Steps	Responsi-ble Person	Team Mem-bers	Measured by:	Due Date	Sta-tus
Develop Disciple-ship Pro-grams*	Identify teaching topics.	Pastor Joe Smith	Susan Jones	Completion by due date	March 1st	
	Research curricu-lum.	Susan Jones	Susan Jones	Completion by due date	April 15th	
	Identify teachers.	Pastor Joe Smith	Susan Jones	Completion by due date	April 30th	
	Schedule classes	Susan Jones	Susan Jones	Completion by due date	May 15th	

*This goal supports the organizational goal of increasing attendance by 10%. It also supports the strategic goal of increasing church attendance to 1500 congregants. Developing discipleship programs was identified by congregant feedback and the hope is if done well, congregants will want to bring people to church for the experience.

5. Employee Goals

To ensure that the departmental goals are accomplished, they need to be driven down to the individual employee/volunteer level. This is done by identifying the steps the employee needs to take in order to accomplish the goals. As you will note, these goals line up with the individual's departmental goals.

This goal document is a valuable tool during the annual performance appraisal process because it helps to ensure that what the organization wanted to accomplish at the beginning of the year was completed. Departmental goals should be delegated to employees within the department to share the responsibility for getting things done.

Some churches don't have employees but may use volunteers to help accomplish goals. The more people who help, and have accountability for achieving goals, the more achievable the implementation becomes. Now we will take the above departmental goal and break it down into steps for an employee or volunteer to accomplish.

Objective (goal)	Action Steps	Responsible Person	Team Members	Measured by:	Due Date	Status
1.Research Discipleship curriculum	1. Benchmark other like churches 2. Internet research 3. Interview pastors and members 4. Review ideas with Pastor Smith 5. Order curriculum for classes	Susan Jones	Pastor Joe Smith	Accomplished by due date	April 15	In process
2.Schedule Classes	1. Identify available classrooms 2.Schedule classrooms 3. Advertise classes in bulletin, website, etc. 4.Register attendees 5.Solicit class evaluations 6.Summarize evaluations 7.Enter attendees in database	Susan Jones	Pastor Joe Smith	Accomplished by due date	April 30	In process

As you will notice the objective (goal) for Susan is taken from the action steps in the departmental goal. This allows Pastor Joe Smith to assign responsibility to Susan Jones for accomplishing this goal. This document will be used when Susan is reviewed at her annual performance appraisal which will demonstrate her goal completion. By Susan completing her goal, it allows Pastor Joe Smith to accomplish his goals, which supports the overall church goals.

6. Job Description

A church employee's or volunteer job description should include their goal responsibilities and be updated annually. This helps to ensure that the job description is accurate. Job descriptions should be written to reflect individual goals which support the departmental goals as well as reporting relationship (this is to identify who the boss is).

The document should also list job duties that this person is responsible for. Job descriptions should be reviewed and updated annually (performance appraisal time is a good time to do this).

7. Performance Appraisals

The performance appraisal process should be a time to reflect on the last year and celebrate successes. It should also be used as a time to course correct if an employee has gotten off track. Reinforcing the positive and celebrating the successes can influence future positive behaviors.

A structured performance management process incorporates annual goals into the employee performance appraisal and holds employees accountable for completing those goals that support church strategy.

Churches that invest the time clarifying their mission and vision, and develop a strategic plan that disseminates goals throughout the ministry, not only experience success at implementing the plan, but also engages employees and volunteers to support the mission of the organization. This kind of engagement is how God uses the body to build the church!

Practical Application Exercises

1. Does your church have a mission statement, vision statement and list of core values? If so, identify them. Otherwise, draft a set that best captures the priorities of your church.

2. Utilizing what you know about mission statements, vision and core values compose your own person credos statement.

3. In your own words, define:

      a. Mission statement
      b. Vision statement
      c. Core values
      d. Strategy Plan

Recommended Resources for Further Study

Ansbro, John J., The Credos of Eight Black Leaders: Converting Obstacles into Opportunities. University Press of America, 2005. (ISBN 978-0-761-83214-0)

Barna, George, The Power of Vision: Discover and Apply God's Plan for Your Life and Ministry. Baker Books, 2009. (ISBN 978-1-441-22362-3)

Gentile, Yvonne & Cartmill, Carol, Leadership Essentials: Practical Tools for Leading in the Church. Abingdon Press, 2006. (ISBN 978-1-426-76242-0)

King, Dr. Jeanne Porter, Building Church A Church Full of Leaders: A Guide for Unleashing the Leadership Potential of Your Church. Life to Legacy LLC, 2014. (ISBN 978-1-939-65422-9)

Malphurs, Aubrey, Developing a Vision for Ministry. Baker Books, 2015. (ISBN 978-1-493-40040-9)

Malphurs, Aubrey, The Dynamics of Church Leadership (Ministry Dynamics for a New Century). Baker Books, 1999. (ISBN 978-1-441-23173-4)

McMullen, Shawn, Unleashing the Potential of the Smaller Church: Vision and Strategy for Life-changing Ministry. Standard Publishing, 2006. (ISBN 978-0-784-71621-2)

Church Growth

Growing a church requires a vision, thought and strategy. Successful churches are those that follow a God-given vision and mission, define the steps to get there and implement their strategic plan.

The beauty of the body of Christ is that God uses everyone in a slightly different way and those unique qualities, that each church possesses, is what God uses to create a beautiful tapestry of churches.

Church growth is not about competing with the ministry down the street but more about developing the people God has planted in the local church to be used by God with their unique gifts. I believe that people are called to churches for a specific purpose. We are all on a journey and the church helps us develop as Christians and supports our unique calling.

Rick Warren wrote "...since the church is a living organism, it is natural for it to grow if it is health...if a church is not growing it is dying..." This can be a scary concept for a small local church. With growth comes many challenges but the exciting thing is that with God ALL things are possible and He gives wisdom freely!

There is a theory that some churches fail to grow – thrive – because the leadership gets comfortable with the way things are and doesn't do anything to change the status quo. This may be ok – but it may not be. Could it be that there are people who could benefit from a particular church body that is stagnant? In this chapter, we will discover seven keys to church growth.

1. Know Where the Church is Going

There is an old adage "if you fail to plan, you plan to fail." This is true in business as well as churches. Having a well-defined vision, mission and values statement sets the direction for any organization and developing a strategic plan to map out the steps to get there is how a vision is achieved.

People are drawn to a compelling mission and vision and get excited about being a part of an organization that is making a difference! It is exciting when a church member can share stories of the early days and celebrate the journey of how the church matured, developed and grew.

2. Create an Inviting Atmosphere

It is unfortunate, but true, that we are a consumer driven society and people are naturally drawn to an aesthetically appealing environment. People like to be proud of where they worship so providing an environment that is comfortable, clean and orderly is important. Paying attention to things like clean, stocked restrooms, clean glass surfaces and freshly vacuumed carpeting can go a long way in creating a comfortable atmosphere for members and guests.

3. Create a Welcoming Experience

There are not many things as awkward for a church visitor as to be ignored or to be overwhelmed with attention. Everyone wants to be greeted but not everyone is comfortable being inundated with unwelcome attention.

Try to remember that most people who visit a church are looking for something – time with God. They might be exploring the Christian faith for the first time or checking to see if the church culture is a good fit. Regardless, it is important to make the experience as positive as possible.

There is a tender balance between creating a welcoming experience and an awkward one. But, with socially skilled people and a little training it can be done.

4. Care for Church Members

Church members are one of the key customer groups in a church. Understanding their unique needs and ensuring their needs are met – within the scope of the vision – is critical to church growth.

For example, if the church has volunteer opportunities, make sure the application and communication process is a good experience. Or if a volunteer is given a job or responsibility, try to make sure they know what is expected of them and have what they need to do their job. The goal is to provide the support for their needs.

Having said that, there are people who sometimes make unreasonable demands for things that don't line up with the vision or strategy of the church and can be difficult to deal with. I recall a pastor friend who would respond to this kind of person with "either love me or leave me but don't stay here and fight me…" Some people are unreasonable and you need to just let them move on.

5. Provide Opportunities to Serve

At the core of all of us is a desire to serve others. Jesus did it and as Christians we need to be provided with opportunities to help other people. So whether it is serving meals to the less fortunate, organizing mission trips, or helping others in a time of crisis – opportunities to serve offers members the chance to use their gifts to help God's people. A well-defined strategic plan can help identify the kinds of service opportunities that support the vision of the church.

6. Proper Management of Church Resources

God provides financial resources to churches and there is responsibility that comes with managing those resources. Churches that are good stewards of ministry funds, and are diligent with their budgeting processes, are better prepared financially for the needs of expanding facilities, updating equipment and other necessities to operate a church.

There needs to be good oversight and management of God's money! God's money is the most important money in the world to manage well! Being a good steward of ministry funds is an important responsibility of the call.

7. Enjoy the Ride

Whether you are the senior pastor, a business administrator or a church secretary, the call should be enjoyable, fulfilling and balanced. Spending time with God is what fuels the call and the anointing to do what needs to be done in a church. I remember this one quote I read some time ago "Don't get so caught up in the ministry of the Lord that we forget the Lord of the Ministry."

If God called you into ministry, don't take that call lightly, spend time with Him and He will instruct you in the way you should go! If you take that instruction, write the vision down and map out a plan to get there – biblical church growth is inevitable!

Practical Application Exercises

1. Prepare a 3-paragraph essay summarizing the key components of this chapter and its overall importance to church administration.

Recommended Resources for Further Study

Exman, Gary W., Get Ready—Get Set—Grow!: Church Growth for Town and Country Congregations. CSS Publishing, 1987. (ISBN 978-0-895-36865-2)

McGavran, Donald A., Understanding Church Growth. Wm. B. Eerdmans Publishing, 1990. (ISBN 978-0-802-80463-1)

McIntosh, Gary L., Biblical Church Growth: How You Can Work with God to Build a Faithful Church. Baker Books, 2003. (ISBN 978-0-801-09156-8)

Rainer, Thom S., The Book of Church Growth. B&H Publishing Group, 1998. (ISBN 978-1-733-66946-0)

Wagner, C. Peter, Your Church Can Grow: Seven Vital Signs of a Healthy Church. Wipf and Stock Publishers, 2001. (ISBN 978-1-579-10589-1)

Wagner, C. Peter, Towns, Elmer L. & Rainer, Thom S., <u>The Everychurch Guide to Growth: How Any Plateaued Church Can Grow</u>. B&H Publishing Group, 1998. (ISBN 978-1-433-67494-5)

Church Constitution & By-laws

Every church needs an updated Constitution and by-laws. This governing document sets forth what the church has agreed on so that it may run effectively. If your church's Constitution and Bylaws document has not been reviewed and updated within the past two or three years, now is a good time to give it a good look. In most instances, when a church is taken to court, the court will look to the organization's bylaws to determine whether that church and its' leaders have acted within the scope of their duties. The set of bylaws is the organization's most important document for legal purposes because it details the internal workings of the church.

It is vital that this document be prepared properly and that it include all the protections available for the church to safeguard it against many of the lawsuits that are being filed against religious orders today. Courts in the U.S. generally contend that a member who joins a church with knowledge of the bylaws has agreed to be bound by the bylaws—even to those with which they may disagree. The members that are to be subject to the bylaws should either be given a personal copy or informed as to where they may review these bylaws.

The existence and the accuracy of the document are legally imperative to protect a church's tax-exempt status. Since no two churches operate the same way, the constitution should be written to reflect each church's specific needs and practices. At a minimum, it should include general provisions on:

Name and purpose.

The purpose statement should be so broad in scope that it covers both present active ministries and potential future ministries. In addition, to protect the church's tax-exempt status under Section 501(c) (3) of the federal tax code, the ministry purpose must (1) be religious, charitable, scientific, testing, for public safety, literary or educational; and (2) not involve the church in partisan political campaigns or substantial legislative activity.

Statement of faith

It is critical that the church constitution state clearly and unequivocally what the church believes as a matter of Biblical faith. The constitution should indicate that the Bible controls all church matters. It is also wise to establish which version of the Bible the church will use as its official standard. Including the statement of faith in the constitution will help safeguard the church from drifting toward liberalism, and strengthens it against encroachment from false teaching. Your statement of faith should touch on all the major teachings of the Bible and should set forth the church's position relating to each one. Be sure to include the biblical references for each item covered.

In addition, some social issues create more litigation than others, so it has become necessary for churches to declare in writing their positions on such issues as homosexuality, same-sex marriage and abortion. McNamara provides the following sample statement concerning marriage and family:

"We believe God ordained marriage and the family as the foundational institution of human society, and that the only legitimate marriage is a sacred and permanent covenant relationship between one man and one woman, symbolizing the union of Christ and his Church. The husband is to be the servant leader in the home and is to love his wife as Christ loves the church, and the wife is to submit herself to the Scriptural leadership of her husband as the church submits to the headship of Christ (Genesis 2:18-25; Matthew 19:4-6; Ephesians 5:22-25)."

McNamara continues by providing the following sample statement concerning human sexuality:

"We believe God has commanded that no intimate sexual activity is to be engaged in outside of the marriage of a man and a woman. Any form of child molestation, fornication, adultery, homosexuality, lesbianism, bestiality, incest, pedophilia, or pornography is a sinful perversion of God's gift of sex. We believe God disapproves of and forbids any attempt to alter one's gender by surgery or appearance. (Genesis 2:22-24; 19:5, 13; Leviticus 18:1-30; Matthew 19:4-6; Romans 1:26-29; 7:2; First Corinthians 5:1; 6:9; Galatians 3:28; Ephesians 5:22-23; First Thessalonians 4:1-8; Hebrews 13:4)"

Membership qualifications

The church constitution should clearly define the qualifications for church membership. It is also legally imperative that a termination provision for church membership be included as well. For example, automatic removal from memberships rolls any person (other than college students, military personnel, shut-ins, missionaries or evangelists) who has not attended a regular church service in the preceding six months. The Christian Law Association discourages the use of an "inactive member" status.

Membership rights and disputes

The church constitution should clearly state that members have no contract, property or civil legal rights in the property or other ministry affairs of the church. This provision is important for churches seeking to maintain their tax-exempt status. Section 501(c) (3) of the federal tax code provides that no part of the net earnings of a tax-exempt organization may inure to the benefit of any private shareholder or individual.

A provision is needed to demonstrate how personal disputes between a church member and the church will be resolved. Based on 1 Corinthians 6:1-8, this provision should limit the resolution of disputes between brethren to a Biblically based Christian process and restrict access to litigation in the civil courts. Thus, the church constitution should provide that "all members of this church agree to submit to binding arbitration any matters which cannot otherwise be resolved, and expressly waive any and all rights in law and equity to bringing any civil disagreement before a court of law."

Church officer selection and authority

The church constitution should include how the pastor and deacons or other church officers are selected, their terms of office and so on. At minimum, the church corporation needs to have a president, a secretary and a treasurer. If other titles are preferred—such as pastor or deacon—the church constitution needs to identify the corporate function of the ministry name. (For instance, the pastor is generally stated to be the president of the corporation.)

The church constitution should also address the procedures for nominating and electing officers, the terms of service for each officer, their duties, the procedure for removing an officer before the end of his elected term, and the procedure for filling a vacancy if an officer's full term is not served.

The church leadership should be given sufficient authority to effectively lead and conduct the ministries of the church. It is unwise to create such an elaborate set of checks and balances that none of the church leadership has sufficient liberty to do anything on behalf of the church and its ministries.

An official spokesman for the church should also be expressly designated. If for some reason the church comes to the attention of the media or a government entity, there should be no confusion as to who in the church may speak on its behalf.

Licensing or ordination

The church constitution should set forth the qualifications for a candidate for licensing or ordination as a minister of the Gospel as stated in 1 Timothy 3:1-7 and Titus 1:6-9. A procedure for how and whether the candidate should be presented to the church for licensing or ordination should also be established.

Meetings

The church constitution should provide for the frequency and location of meetings. Separate sections should be written for meetings for worship and meetings for church administration. The worship section should cover meetings for public worship, Bible study and prayer, and the time for observing the ordinance of the Lord's Supper. The administration section should cover regular, special and annual meetings for the conduct of church business. This section should also define the ministry's fiscal year.

It is important that the church constitution carefully dictate the rules and procedures for all church administration meetings. This procedure should include:
- Frequency of regular meetings;
- What constitutes a forum;
- The practice of opening and closing meetings with prayer;

- Who is to serve as moderator or preside at meetings;
- The order of business on the agenda;
- The process for calling special meetings; and
- Setting the annual meeting date.

Although many churches adopt *Robert's Rules of Order* for parliamentary procedure, many groups contend it is preferable for the church to create its own workable rules based upon the Bible and common sense.

Church discipline

A church that intends to exercise church discipline must have the Biblical guidelines for doing so carefully outlined in its constitution. Specific reference to governing Scriptures is recommended (i.e., Matthew 18:15-20; 1 Corinthians 5:1-13; Galatians 6:1; 1 Thessalonians 5:14; 2 Thessalonians 3:6, 10-15; 1 Timothy 5:19-20; and Titus 3:10-11).

Discipline guidelines should provide the steps for approaching an offending party with the goal of restoration. The guidelines should also provide for a hearing before a discipline committee with a recommendation to the church members providing an ongoing opportunity for repentance and restoration. In case of members who are unwilling to repent, a process for removal from church membership should also be included in the disciple guidelines. Once these guidelines are established, they should be meticulously followed when exercising church discipline.

Financial matters

The church constitution should contain a provision specifying who may authorize an unbudgeted expenditure, and what amount may be expended without special authorization.

Contributions designated by the contributor for a specific purpose impose a "trust" obligation upon the recipient church to use the funds for that purpose only. To avoid being required to ask the donor for permission to use the funds for a purpose other than the designated purpose, the constitution should contain a specific provision making a gift designation advisory rather than mandatory in nature. This would allow all designated contributions to remain subject to the exclusive control and discretion of the pastor and the Board of Deacons.

Amendments

It is important that a church constitution provide for an amendment process. This allows the church to be flexible in addressing new concerns and developments. Churches should make the amendment process simple. Typically, the provision should provide for "a majority vote of the members present and voting at any regular church administration meeting." In addition, notice of the proposed amendment must be submitted in writing within a specified number of days before the vote is taken.

WHAT IS A CHURCH CONSTITUTION?

The Constitution is the workhorse of a church's governing documents. It deals with the principles, offices, accountabilities, and procedures of congregational life. There are four realities that must be kept in mind as you develop this vital document:

A Church Constitution if a Polity Manual

"Polity" refers to a particular form or system of governance. It describes where the authority with the group resides and who makes the final decisions. The form of church government is tremendously important for both the harmony and the permanency of the church and its testimony. There are basically four major styles of church polity.

1) Authority resides in the hands of a single leader.
2) Authority resides in the hands of an elite few outside the local church.
3) Authority resides in the hands of elected representatives.
4) Authority resides in the hands of the members.

Baptists have long held that congregational rule with strong pastoral leadership is the only biblical form of polity taught in the New Testament. Churches are not democracies patterned after Western-style civics. Instead, they are congregational in nature with the ultimate authority for decision making residing in the people themselves. As found in Acts 6:1, churches follow a democratic-representative approach to get things done.

To ensure that things are "done decently and in order," churches develop written documents known as "constitutions" which prescribe a congregational form of governance, the requirements and rules for membership, the standards and responsibilities of leadership, and the procedures for conducting the affairs of the church. These documents supply the agreed-upon ground rules for everyone involved in the local church and often prescribe the parliamentary procedures that secure the right of the majority to decide while giving the minority a voice to be heard.

We must be careful never to elevate these procedures, or the constitution itself, above the dictates of God's Holy Word, the Bible. The Word of God is the supreme authority by which all decisions and actions must be evaluated. The church constitution, however, is the polity manual that sets forth the church's understanding of the biblical form of church governance.

A Church Constitution is a Governing Document

Above all else, the church's constitution is a governing document. It tells what can and cannot be done. It explains how the affairs of the church are to be conducted and how the church is to function. It brings civility to business meetings, reigns in unbiblical behavior, curbs the lust for power and control, and protects the rights of both pastor and people.

Without a written document regulating its conduct, a church will soon dissolve into a seething cauldron of competing interest and abusive behavior. The heart of even the most saintly person is still filled with hidden deceit and the potential for untold wickedness. It cannot be trusted. It must be regulated if we are to relate to one another in a biblical fashion. A church constitution helps to do that.

The church constitution contains rules, regulations, and guidelines that both mandate and curtail certain behaviors. Church constitutions are both restrictive and liberating. They curtail our ability to acquire power or to take advantage of our position. They reduce our options to misuse or abuse our authority. They restrict the opportunity for us to engage in unethical behavior.

A church constitution simply provides the structure that governs how any particular church will function in fulfilling its purpose and carrying out its mission here on earth. Human nature soon self-destructs without something to regulate its conduct. The church constitution is a mutually-agreed-upon means for governing the local Body of Christ to which we belong.

A Church Constitution is a Binding Document

Membership in a local church is strictly a voluntary relationship between the individual and the church. People are free to apply for membership whenever they want and are free to leave whenever they want. It should be noted that once a person is accepted into membership he comes under the governing authority of the church—namely its constitution. As a member he is no longer free to do as he wishes. He is now responsible to abide by the principles and policies outlined in this document.

A Church Constitution is a Legal Document

It may come as a surprise to some, but one reason a church constitution is binding upon its pastor and people is because it is a legal document, especially if the church is incorporated. Documents do not need to be drawn up by lawyers and signed by a court judge to be legal documents. Any time an individual or group of individuals reach a contractual agreement (for example, church constitution) and commit themselves to abide by its terms, it becomes legally binding upon them.

Countless court cases have demonstrated the legal nature of church constitutions. Churches are sued for violating provisions of their own constitutions. Pastors and deacons cannot be removed from office except in keeping with the terms of the church constitution. Members cannot be disciplined except in strict compliance with the procedures outlined in the church's governing documents. Monies cannot be transferred from designated funds except in the manner prescribed in the constitution. Accounting procedures disclosed in the church's policy manual must be adhered to. Otherwise, someone may be held accountable in a court of law.

The purpose of a church constitution is to protect the rights of the membership and its leaders. If it weren't for the fact that men's hearts are deceitful and untrustworthy we wouldn't need constitutions. But the reality is that we do have hearts that cannot be trusted, and therefore must be regulated if we are to function in a biblical manner.

WHY DO WE NEED A CONSTITUTION

The fact that church constitutions are not specifically mentioned in Scripture does not preclude their use in our churches today. We have multiple institutions in our churches that are not mentioned directly in scripture but still play a prominent role in our churches today. Church constitutions are both Scriptural and necessary. Here are some reasons why a church needs a written constitution to guide it:

1) *A written constitution complies with Paul's biblical injunction in First Corinthians 14:40 to do all things decently and in order.* In other words, the church is to function in a fair, honest, biblical fashion, and in a civilized and respectful manner.

2) *A written constitution ensures the rights of both the majority and the minority.* The minority is to abide by the will of the majority while the majority is to respect the views of the minority. This is the collective expression of the will of God.

3) *A written constitution protects the church from abuse and harm.*

4) *A written constitution insures that proper procedures are followed.* A written constitution outlines the parliamentary procedures that are to be followed in conducting the affairs of the church and thus helps us avoid all appearance of evil (I Thessalonians 5:22).

5) *A written constitution clarifies the lines of authority, responsibility, and accountability.* The church constitution sets forth the roles, responsibilities, and authority of both the leaders and the laity.

6) *A written constitution instills confidence in the public and members alike.* A well-written, well-thought-out constitution that is consistently and graciously followed by all will go a long ways in restoring confidence in local churches.

7) *A written constitution sets the standard of practice for decades to come.*

SOME MISTAKES TO AVOID WHEN WRITING THE CONSTITUTION

There are several mistakes you want to avoid when writing a church constitution:

1) *Don't spend too much time researching, writing, and rewriting your constitution.* No matter how hard you try you will not be able to produce the "perfect" church constitution.

Throughout the course of ministry, you will discover areas that you did not address adequately in the constitution or some provisions are too limiting or restrictive. These can be addressed through the normal procedures outlined in your constitution.

2) ***Don't simply copy another church's constitution.*** The temptation is when you find a good constitution that works well for another church, simply to adopt it as your own. Young ministers just starting out are especially tempted to copy their home church's constitution. Your church is not the same as your home church or any other church and will be unique in its own right. Write a constitution that fits you and the ministry to which God has called you.

3) ***Don't be too vague.*** Some constitution writers mistakenly use general terms which can be interpreted in several ways. If it is not clear and specific, the people may interpret the constitution to mean something entirely different than was intended originally. If there is fog in the pulpit, there will be fog in the pew. It is vital that you use terminology that is clear, precise, and unambiguous in your constitution. Use plain words that a normal working person with a general education can understand.

4) ***Don't build bottlenecks into the constitution.*** Avoid writing a constitution which allows you to control most of the aspects of the church's ministry where everything has to flow through you. This is a lack of trust both in the Lord and the people, and may be a reflection on your

failure to adequately disciple and equip people for ministry.

5) ***Don't think you can avoid future change.*** Understand that change is inevitable. You cannot stop it from happening, although may attempt to do so by using restrictive terminology in their constitutions. It is far better to write a good, solid constitution with flexibility built into it that allows for appropriate change as the church grows, and then work hard to instill those values, standards and beliefs into the hearts and minds of the people.

IMPLEMENTING AND ABIDING BY THE CHURCH'S CONSTITUTION

A church constitution is merely a blueprint outlining how a church is supposed to function. The constitution committee—like an architect—draws up the diagram and then presents it to the people for their approval and adoption. Having adopted the constitution, the church must now begin to implement its provisions.

Implementing the Constitution

Time is required for a constitution to take hold and to begin functioning as planned. A church may not be able to implement all of its provisions immediately. Qualified people may not be available to fill all the positions outlined in the constitution. There may not be any godly men who meet the biblical requirements for being deacons. Key leadership position may have to be left empty. Whatever you do—do no fill those positions with people who are not spiritually qualified. It is better to leave positions unfilled than to place someone in a leadership position that should not be there.

The constitution takes effect immediately upon approval, even though you may not be able to fill all the positions outlined therein. Financial procedures will need to be brought into conformity with the requirements of the constitution. You may need to apply for admittance to a particular fellowship or association of churches (if mandated in the constitution). Read through the constitution and note the things it requires which are not now being done, and then take steps to start doing those things.

One of the most important things you will need to do is review the church's mission statement, and evaluate your current ministry in light of your mission statement. Which aspects of your mission are you currently fulfilling? Which ones are missing? What changes in the current program need to be made? What needs to be implemented? Remember, "mission" is what your church is supposed to be doing, not necessarily what it is doing. You may need to discontinue some of the things you are doing in order to start doing some of the things you should be doing.

Policy and Procedures Manual

Consider developing a Policies and Procedures manual. This is a living, evolving document that describes how the various principles and requirements found in the constitution are implemented in the daily life of the church. It should also include various practices, standards, positions, and procedures not specifically mentioned in the constitution such as music standards, vacation policies, etc. It outlines disciplinary procedures, hiring and termination guidelines, job descriptions, performance evaluations, travel policies, etc.

Rather waiting until a problem arises, the P&P manual determines in advance how a matter is to be handled. This avoids a great deal of heartache, pain, and anguish for all concerned. It builds confidence because people know what to do and what is expected. People will have greater confidence in the leaders of the church because they know they are well organized and have carefully thought through policy and procedural issues. It helps people focus in the same direction while avoiding conflict and enables you to say "no" to suggestions and ideas that would hinder or undermine the effectiveness of the church.

The P&P manual is a growing document. Each time a new policy or procedure is implemented, it is added to the manual. The manual should always be kept in the church office and should be available to the public upon request. It should be clearly understood that no individual (including a pastor or deacon) can change the policy manual to suit himself. Policies and procedures should be adopted either by the congregation itself or approved by the church council. Because the policy manual is mandated in the its constitution, its provisions have the same authority and weight as any other provision of the constitution, and must be followed by everyone in the church.

Abiding by the Provisions of the Constitution

A good constitution is no good if its provisions are ignored or held in contempt. It has value and force only when its constituents honor and abide by it. Many churches have good constitutions, but they don't follow them. Membership requirements are ignored, financial guidelines are nullified, leadership qualifications are disregarded, and as a result abuse is often perpetrated.

Church constitutions sometimes suffer from benign neglect. Other times, they are blatantly torn asunder by dictatorial leaders who refuse to be "hampered" by a piece of paper. If you are going to a biblical church that functions under the authority of the New Testament, then you must follow the principles outlined in the New Testament. That means you will follow a congregational form of church polity. It is the congregation, and not the pastor, who ultimately decides how the biblical principles outlined in Scripture are going to be implemented in that particular church. Those decisions take form most often in the church's constitution. The pastor is the leader, but ultimate authority resides with the congregation.

Practical Application Exercises

1. Draft a sample church constitution for your church ensuring to follow the guidelines outlined in this chapter.

Recommended Resources for Further Study

Brand, Chad & Norman, Stan (ed.), <u>Perspectives on Church Government</u>. B&H Publishing Group, 2004. (ISBN 978-1-433-66914-9)

Engle, Paul E. & Cowan, Steven B., <u>Who Runs the Church?: 4 Views on Church Government</u>. Harper Collins, 2009. (ISBN 978-0-310-54352-7)

Foshee, Howard, <u>Broadman Church Manual</u>. B&H Publishing Group, 1973. (ISBN 978-1-433-67534-8)

Goncharenko, Simon Victor, <u>Church Government According to the Bible</u>. Wipf and Stock Publishers, 2014. (ISBN 978-1-630-87438-4)

Heward-Mills, Dag, <u>Church Administration and Management</u>. WestBow Press, 2001. (ISBN 978-1-449-71253-2)

Mather, Richard, <u>Church Government and Church Covenant Discussed</u>. Literary Licensing LLC, 2014. (ISBN 978-1-497-96898-1)

Turner, William Clair, <u>Discipleship for African American Christians: A Journey through the Church Covenant</u>. Judson Press, 2002. (ISBN 978-0-817-01434-6)

Church Financial Administration

I really do not believe that any book on church administration would be complete without a chapter devoted to the finances of the church. The mere mention of church administration prompts the average person to think of finances. Administering the financial resources of the church is a tremendously important part of being effective in our ministry.

Let's face it. Money plays an important role in the lives of individuals and families, and even more so in the church. The acquisition of financial resources represents the compilation of hard work, creative thought, discipline, and thrift. But what are these financial resources. Tidwell offered this definition: *Financial resources are the money, the knowledge, the skills, the attitudes, the commitment, which whelp make available those human and physical resources needed to implement the ministries of a church.*

The spending of money signifies a church's values and priorities. Someone who is ignorant about a church would be able to describe that church's priorities fairly accurately simply by analyzing its budget and financial information. Their analysis will often begin by determining whether a majority of members are contributing to the church financially. Other questions to be considered are: Is the church spending money to meet needs in the community in addition to providing for its own upkeep? Is the church spending money on youth ministry and education? The answers to these questions and others will be suggested by the general operating budget.

It is crucial that members and the community have complete trust in the integrity of the church's financial system. It is of extreme importance when administering the church's resources that we remember that these belong to God—not us—to be utilized to his honor through ministry. In effect, we are called to be good stewards of God's resources. This requires that we make the effort to understand financial realities as they relate to the ministry of the church. It further requires the commitment to faithfully manage such resources.

Administrative Responsibilities Regarding Money

There are several major administrative responsibilities for the church to consider with regard to the money. This author chooses to note that this list is in no wise to be considered all-inclusive and special care should be taken on the part of the reader to perform the necessary further research.

Effective Leaders in Administration are Kept Informed of Financial State

The pastor is ultimately responsible for everything that happens in the church. There should be nothing he or she does not know or is kept abreast of. This is especially true with regard to the financial resources of the church. While the pastor is never to handle the church's cash, the pastor is obliged to ensure—usually through the finance committee—that policies are set and followed for the proper handling of money. Many pastors have witnessed sharp declines in attendance and giving following the mere hint of mishandling of funds. Unfortunately for some, the sole person held responsible in these situations is the pastor for having not ensured proper safeguards were in place. There is some good news for the pastor though. Although pastoral oversight is required, this aspect of administration only demands a small portion of the pastor's time.

What if a new pastor reports to a new church and these safeguards aren't already in place? Would this not be a sensitive subject for the new pastor to tackle? It is true that when we attempt to make the necessary changes, many in the church will view it as we are impugning the wisdom of the finance committee or the integrity of those who handle the money. Those individuals who count the money usually hold more clout than an incoming pastor and are many times very intimidating. However, if something was to go amiss with the church's finances, it is the pastor and not the chair of the finance committee who will be cumbered with the blame. Since it is our head on the block, we are wise to ensure that proper procedures for the handling of money are followed.

When addressing the absence of these needed safeguards, it would be wise to let your financial leaders know that these are not your ideas but standard practice in many churches. There are many books on the subject of church finances that you might consider sharing with you financial leaders. Many times when people are educated on a standard, they are usually apt to make necessary corrections. In the event that the financial leaders refuse to adopt the principles, you may consider drafting the policies as a recommendation and having them entered into the archives of the finance committee and church council. Be sure to keep a copy in your personal files as evidence that you attempted to fulfill your leadership obligation with due diligence.

The pastor should know about *every* aspect of the church's finances. You should know everything the treasurer, financial secretary, and finance chair know. You should know about all regular, special and reserve accounts to include the balances, financial institutions, and any designations on the accounts. The pastor should also know what obligations the church has to federal, state, and local governments in addition to who is employed by the church and their salaries. You do not have to memorize the budget and financial information; however, you should be thoroughly familiar with every aspect of the finances and be able to put your hands on the information quickly.

Church Administrators Need Develop an Adequate Perspective about Money

Tidwell stated that this may very well be the most difficult part of the whole subject. It is the most abstract dimension of finance administration being that it involves theological concepts while reaching into the psychological. It affects the spiritual realm while call-

ing for a variety of skills. It surfaces in attitude atti-
tudes and behavior and requires systematic, procedural
attention and diligence. Simply, it is a very complex
place at which to begin.

It is becoming common practice that some well-
intended layperson will advise a new pastor, that if the
pastor would take care of the "spiritual," the laity
would take care of the "temporal." No doubt that in
some instances the lay person means to relieve the pastor of the burden of bothering with the finances.
However, in other instances the layperson means to
advise the pastor to stay out of the church's financial
business. Some have even been bold enough to instruct the pastor not to preach about finances. All of
these notions represent inadequate perspectives about
money.

Sometimes the most spiritual thing one might do is to
manage money correctly. The spiritual and the temporal are too closely intertwined to be separated. The
way a minister leads a church in its temporal affairs
might be one of the strongest spiritual dimensions of
all.

Some things to note when developing an adequate perspective about money would include:
1. Jesus frequently referred to money
2. A Christian view of material things is basic
3. Sermons about stewardship are an effective
   way to develop the needed perspective about
   money in the church.

Effective Administration Hinges on Budget Development

A budget is a comprehensive financial plan that reflects the specific amounts of money allocated from anticipated income for supporting the church's ministries and related expenses for a definite period of time, usually a year. It is a guide that helps to manage expenses and revenues in the most effective and efficient manner. Budgets should not be viewed merely in terms of cold, hard numbers seeing that they communicate a church's priorities. A budget is a communication tool. It forces people to talk, exchange ideas, and modify plans when necessary.

Many people instinctively think of budgeting only as it relates to planning for the future. However, one cannot plan effectively for the future without first understanding the past, which conveys the church's financial position in the present. The budget ought to consist in part of an organized summary of what the church has done in the past. A church would therefor need to keep a careful, detailed record of all income and expenditures. While many churches do a good job at maintaining accurate records, they often times fail to make effective use of it. Financial officers may even neglect to share this information with church leaders. A thorough understanding of this information is imperative in the planning of the church's budget by leadership.

The most common type of budget is the line-item budget. In this specific kind of budget, there is an allocation for each type of item for which there is antici-pated expenditure, without regard for the particular activity or ministry the item supports (i.e., postage, lit-erature, salaries, missions, benevolence, paper, socials, missions). This kind of budget has often been referred to as an accountant's format. Its simplicity permits for the composition of a budget to be completed quickly. The previous year's budget, plus some projected ad-justments in estimates related to each line item, would give you the new budget. Many churches have been satisfied with the use of this process. For more infor-mation on this type of budgeting, one could refer to *The Church Finance Record System Manual* by Marvin Crowe and Merrill Moore published in 1959 by the Broadman Press.

There is another type of budget that is growing in pop-ularity among churches known as ministry-action budgeting. In this type of budgeting, the budget takes the shape of major church programs. Budget requests as related to church programs are arranged according to their estimated priority in meeting needs compatible with the church's purpose and objectives. This system leads the church to view the budget as a prioritized package of ministry actions to be carried out by the church. For more information regarding this type of budgeting, refer to the book *Christian Stewardship in Action* or Tidwell's *Church Administration—Effective Leadership for Ministry*.

Although it takes approximately ten weeks to com-pose, church leaders may wish to experiment with ministry-action budgeting. It offers far more motiva-

tional potential than does the line-item budget. Ministry-action budgeting informs the members more in
terms of their interest. Church members could be very
interested in what is being accomplished in ministry
and at what cost. One good experience with ministry-
action budgeting would probably convince church
leaders of its value as a tool for financial administration.

Administration Leaders Should Know Where the Money is coming from

Another major administrative responsibility in church
finance is to anticipate the sources of income for the
church. It is important to know how much money the
church might reasonably expect to receive during the
period to be covered by the new budget. A major part
of the work of those who plan the church budget is to
estimate how much money might come in and from
what sources it might be expected to come.

In many churches, the bulk of the money can be expected to come from the undesignated tithes and
offerings of the members. This source might be subdi-
vided to reflect what comes through regular gifts in
church offering envelopes, usually through the Sunday
School, and that which comes as "loose offerings" in
the offering plates during the worship services. Usually smaller proportions come as designated gifts for
special causes. Other sources for some churches include rental fees from properties, memorial gifts,
interest income on money invested, trusts, wills, and
other sources.

The usual way of estimating the income for the next year is to study the patterns of giving for previous years and project the trend into the future. The projection might be the anticipated percentage increase, translated to actual dollars. Other factors might enter into the projection, such as the state of the economy where the church is located and anticipated changes in the membership of the church.

Some things to consider when anticipating the source of income include:
1. Program planners should lead in allocation changes
2. Avoid legally or ethically questionable money-making projects.

Effective Leaders Seek to Secure Commitment to Support the Budget

There are at least half a dozen ways for which there are denominational materials available to help a church in securing commitment of the members to support the budget. Tyson identifies six resources offered through the Southern Baptist Convention Stewardship Services from which church leaders may choose to lead members to support the budget.
1. The Forward Program
2. Alternate Forward Program
3. Committed to Ministries
4. Tithers Commitment Program
5. Stewardship Revival

6. Simplified Church Budget Development and Promotion.

Church leaders should obtain sample materials for the kinds of emphasis they wish to consider. Then they should compare the various program features and choose the one that best suits the needs and readiness of the church. Generally speaking, these plans produce results in keeping with the effort put into them. With some experimenting, leaders can determine what is best for a particular church in getting the members to support the financial plan.

Good Administrators Utilize Orderly Plans for Receiving the Money

The plan should include decisions about using standard envelopes for members' gifts. Income is definitely increased with the use of envelopes. And there are some choices to be made regarding size, color, and manner of distributing the envelopes to the members. Other parts of an adequate plan deal with the system of collecting the offerings, both those that involve the use of envelopes and those that come in other forms.

Any plan needs to afford maximum security for collecting the offering envelopes during Sunday School. Church leaders need to develop a simple standard procedure which includes leaving all envelopes sealed until they reach the point where the official money counters work.

There should be a consistent plan for handling the money received in offering plates during worship services. Do the collectors bring the offering plates to the offering table with or without the money still in them? Where does the money stay until it gets to the official counters? Who is responsible for transferring the money to the counters? These and other questions need to be answered in an adequate plan to fulfill this responsibility of appropriately receiving the money.

Systemize Counting and Banking a Plus

Who will count the money? A committee of no less than three should count the money, although, unfortunately, in most churches one person could actually do the counting. Churches should avoid having a member count the money alone. Leaders should exercise extreme care as they transition from a one-person system of counting, banking, or other aspects of handling church funds.

When will the money be counted? Some counting committees work during the worship services, some immediately after church service, and others return to the church on a day during the week to count. Where will the money rest if there is a delay in counting? And where will the actual counting take place? What procedures will the counting committee follow? These should be written out in checklist fashion and followed with fail. How will you reconcile differences in amounts entered on the outside of offering envelopes and the amounts enclosed in the envelopes?

There are important decisions to make about banking the church's money. Who makes the actual deposits? Where will they be made? When will the money be deposited? Will it be counted before it is deposited, or will it be left in locked bags at the bank for later counting at the bank? Or will be brought back to the church for counting? How many people will accompany the money to and from the bank? Do you need professional security personnel to transport the money? In many churches both the people who handle the money and the money itself are covered by insurance. The people are of more value than the money, and potential threats to their security should be minimized by good procedures.

Record All Monies Received

Whatever method is used to record members' gifts, the records need to be accurately and faithfully kept. Members should receive copies of the record of their gifts, at least annually and preferably each quarter. The shorter interval allows any corrections in the records to be made before the facts get too cold. Assurance that gifts actually reach their intended destinations is important beyond words to members' confidence in the church's handling of money.

The Church Should Utilize Standard Procedures for Requisitioning, Disbursing, and Purchasing

It is beneficial for a church to have a simple yet standard form on which written requests—requisitions—for items which require money are made. This enables the person who is responsible to verify that the item is anticipated in the budget and that there is money available for it at the time requested. Normally, it is not that person's prerogative to deny the request if it is approved in the budget and if there is presently money available to cover the expenditure. When all is in order regarding the requisition, the money can be disbursed for cash purchases, or the purchase can be charged to the church's account for later payment following billing.

The procedures for purchasing need to be determined in a church. It needs to be clear just who is authorized to purchase and how this person is to go about it. Considerable savings can sometimes be realized by buying items which are used in large quantity in larger volumes. Then other questions come such as whether or not there is satisfactory storage and distribution for these items. There are other matters leaders need to work out regarding purchasing. One important matter is to verify that what is received is exactly what was ordered. Other matter include buying wholesale or retail, paying with the order but before receiving the goods purchased, whether to maintain a limit like a thirty-day period following billing for payment to be made, and many others.

Leaders in Church Administration Use Adequate Accounting and Auditing Procedures

The book *Conducting Church Audits—A Guide for Internal Auditors* offers practical help. Leaders can adapt and adopt a system that is tailored to the church's accounting needs. I give a sample procedure which a church audit committee can use to perform an audit of the church's records and finances. An annual audit is recommended, and it should be done by persons who are not involved in handling the church's money or in purchasing or bookkeeping for the church. A committee whose members can do simple arithmetic can perform the audit for the majority of churches. Larger churches may need to pay for a professional audit to be performed. This examination and verification of accounts should be routine rather than only when a concern arises around the church's finances. It is far more valuable to prevent problems than to uncover them after some unfortunate experience. Insisting on an audit also assists in the pastor's and the finance committee's endeavor to practice due diligence when administering the financial resources of the church.

Good Church Administrators Will Report to the Church

Church leaders should inform members of income, expenditures, variances, adjustments, and special opportunities, needs, or problems related to the church's finances. Most churches require a monthly or quarterly report to the church in a business meeting. Almost all churches then have an annual financial report which generally follows the same format as the church budget. Some reports are given in great detail, including the percentages figures represent, how the present report compares with the report for the same time last year, and many other items of information.

How much to report is a matter for each church to determine. Generally speaking, it is better to give a bit more than is required than to give less thereby arousing suspicion that something may be wrong about the finances.

Good administrative leadership with financial resources in a church is vital. Financial resources make up a vital link in the ministry chain. They help to make available the physical resources and support the human resources in performing a church's ministries. Financial resources include more than money, but money is the focus of the administrative ideas in this chapter.

Perhaps more than any other area, irregularity or scandal in the realm of finances can destroy a congregation or a pastor's ministry. But these easily implemented systems can create an environment of transparence and safety for financial procedures. Observing due diligence with church finances is not difficult or complicated, but it is essentially vital.

Practical Application Exercises

1. Prepare a summation of 1,000 words or fewer detailing the need for effective administration of church finances.

2. Write a paragraph in 750 words or slightly less, in which you identify the financial resources of the church.

Recommended Resources for Further Study

Davis, Lee E., In Charge: Managing Money for Christian Living. Broadman Press, 1984. (ISBN 978-0-805-46404-7)

Henry, Jack A., Basic Budgeting for Churches: A Complete Guide. B&H Publishing Group, 1995. (ISBN 978-0-805-46175-6)

Henry, Jack A., Basic Accounting for Churches: A Turnkey Manual. Broadman & Holman, 1994. (ISBN 978-0-805-46145-9)

Nuffer, Bruce, The Church Treasurer's Manual: A Practical Guide for Managing Church Finances. Beacon Hill Press, 2008. (ISBN 978-0-834-12383-0)

Odom, Jeremy W., Conducting Church Audits: A Guide for Internal Auditors. Big O Publishing Group, 2016. (ISBN 978-0-9970-9562-3)

Ray, Cecil, <u>Living the Responsible Life</u>. Carib Baptist Publications, 1983. (ISBN 978-0-311-72371-3)

Toler, Stan, <u>Stewardship Strategies: Sermons, Letters, and Strategies for Promoting Biblical Stewardship</u>. Beacon Hill Press, 1998. (ISBN 978-0-834-11743-3)

How to Conduct Church Meetings

A pastor's wife once asked, "Why would any organization schedule one time a month for Christians to be entirely out of character?" Sadly, the monthly church conference or business meeting is often a time of disorder, distrust, and disruption; however, with a few adjustments, the church conference can be a model of the character of Christ.

A well-managed board actually multiplies the efforts of the pastor and staff in accomplishing the ministry. The pastor/chairman of the business or board meeting must guide the meeting in an orderly manner and maintain an efficient schedule by observing parliamentary rules. The chairman does not dominate the meeting but simply leads the board or congregation through the items of business in a spirit that will bring honor to God's kingdom. It is important that we remember that even though we do all we can to be organized and operate within proper guidelines, we are serving the Lord and His work.

The meeting that conducts the business of the church is a spiritual meeting just as a Bible Study or Sunday service is a spiritual meeting. The focus may be somewhat different, but the conduct of church business is essential to the health and proper functioning of the local church.

John Maxwell states: "Two common problems in board meetings are (1) each person has his own agenda, and (2) the pastor has a difficult time maintaining control of the meeting." Maxwell is right. He recommends avoiding digressions by sticking to an agenda prepared before the meeting. He has a further helpful suggestion of dividing the agenda into three categories: informational, study and action items.

Informational Items

Every meeting should start off on a positive note, and the informational section of the agenda makes this possible. Maxwell recommends including five or six positive reports on the ministry of the church. Use this time to inform and remind of the reason for the meeting. This part of the agenda differs from the "old business/new business" plan, which is usually fruitless, boring, and even negative.

In traditional meetings, finance is the first topic addressed, and unfortunately many meetings never move forward from there. Informational items, on the other hand, are chosen specifically because they are positive, exciting, and set the tone for the rest of the meeting. Spend no more than 5 minutes in this area—just enough time to inspire hearts and prepare them for the most productive segment of the meeting.

Study Items

This part of the agenda always contains the most items. Ninety-five percent of meeting time should be spent studying or discussing these issues and items of interest. Your goal during this part of the meeting is to brainstorm ideas. Work to get every possible suggestion—and objection—on the table.

Never vote on any item that you have listed as a study item. The pressure of a vote causes people to take sides and discourages free and creative thought. Never vote on a study item before the next meeting.

You may keep some study items for months, allowing every option and objection to be put on the table and explored. Other subjects may be study items for only one meeting and then moved on in the next session. Keeping items in the study section of the agenda allows people to process information without feeling threatened, and eventually a consensus is reached. Only then is an item ready to be put before the body for action.

Action Items

The final section of the agenda contains action items, which have already been in the study section for at least one meeting, have already been discussed, and are ready for a vote. Never spend more than 5 minutes in this area. If your board has been candid and the discussion and study have been thorough, there is no reason to spend a lot of time in this section.

If you are currently frustrated by board meetings, you are not alone. Every pastor has been there, and most of us have dreamed of a world without committees. But the truth is we need our board members. They give us perspective, experience, and strength that we don't have alone. A well-managed board actually multiplies the efforts of the pastor and staff in accomplishing the ministry.

The official minutes of a meeting should include (1) the name of the organization, (2) the nature of the meeting—regular or special, (3) time and place, (4) name of the chairman/moderator, (5) the devotional title or topic, (6) correction and approval of previous minutes, (7) business transacted, (8) adjournment, and (9) signature of secretary and date of approval. The pastor may take some liberty in arranging identifying information at the beginning or end of the minutes.

HOW TO CONDUCT A BUSINESS MEETING

Are your church's business meetings low-interest or high-interest events? By giving attention to some basic principles, and by making a commitment to practice them well, you can improve both the quality of your church's business meetings and your ability to lead them.

Establish Your Purpose

Why have church business meetings?

1. Business meetings enable the church to conduct its business in an orderly way. Every church

regularly faces decisions such as these: How shall we spend our money? Which committees will we have and what will be their duties? What will be our church's vision for ministry? Which events will we place on our church's calendar of activities? What are the duties of the church's staff? Business meeting settings facilitate well-thought answers to such questions.

2. Business meetings allow the church an opportunity to discover God's will.

3. Business meetings facilitate better decisions.— "Two heads are better than one," meaning you usually reach a better decision when more than one person has input into the decision. The same truth applies to church business meetings. When you know an item for consideration is going before the church at a business meeting you are more likely to do better fact finding.

4. Business meetings highlight the priesthood of all believers.—As the Lord's priests, we believers have direct access to God. No one individual has a corner up on God's will. A business meeting setting offers those present the privilege of discovering their role and responsibility in the decision being considered. Discussion of motions helps everyone feel they are part of the church, that everyone has equal rights.

Know the Rules and Procedures Your Church has Selected

Your church's constitution and bylaws explains the rights and duties of members, the rules that govern your meetings, and the procedures to be followed for certain decisions. If you are the moderator of your church's business meetings, become familiar with your church's constitution and bylaws document. If your church has no constitution and bylaws, or the existing document needs to be updated, now should be a good time to address this concern.

Your church has likely decided years ago to follow some type of procedure in conducting its meetings. In most cases, the procedure will be to use *Robert's Rules of Order*. Today's revised edition of Robert's Rules of Order serves as a reference guide for conducting meetings of groups and assemblies. We will talk more about these rules later in this chapter.

Understand the Role of the Moderator

In some churches the pastor serves as moderator of church business meetings while in others one of the members functions as moderator. Arguments can be made for and against both of these approaches. The most important question is not who moderates the business meeting, but who can moderate effectively. In many churches a competent layperson functions well as moderator.

The moderator's duties include: (1) developing an agenda for the meeting, (2) conducting the business orderly, (3) maintaining a spirit of fellowship, and (4) clarifying matters voted for later action. The moderator's primary function is to facilitate discussion and to bring together the different views, ideas, and convictions so that a spirit of unit results.

Develop an Agenda for the Business Meeting

Note that there are two types of church business meetings—regular meetings and special meetings. The regular meeting is the standard meeting set for certain times throughout the year. The special meeting is a business meeting called to handle a special request that cannot wait until the regular scheduled business meeting. Advance notice must be given of all special business meetings. Only the item or items that necessitated the call of the special meeting can be considered at a special business meeting.

Here is a sample business meeting agenda for a regular meeting (Note that this is a traditional agenda not as recommended by Maxwell):

- Prayer
- Call to Order
- Report of church clerk
- Reading and approval of minutes from previous meeting(s)
- Approval of requests for letters of church membership

- Treasurer's report
- Reports by various committees
- Handling of motions assigned from a previous meeting
- Handling of motions set for this meeting
- Consideration of new business
- Adjourn

Conduct the Meeting in an Orderly Way

The basic tool for facilitating action at a church business meeting is the motion. All business is conducted by acting on motions. A motion is a formal request that asks the assembly to say or do something. Here is the typical process for handling motions:

1. A member makes a motion.
2. Another member seconds the motion.
3. The moderator repeats the motion to make sure everyone understand it.
4. The members discuss (debate) the motion.
5. The moderator puts the motion to a vote.
6. The moderator announces the result of the vote.

Robert's Rules of Order classifies motions into five classes. The particular class of motion determines its order of precedence and the particular rules governing the use of that motion. In addition, the particular class of the motion determines whether the motion can be used to interrupt the assembly, whether the motion can be discussed or amended, and the type of vote required. In reverse order, the five classes are:

1. Main motions.—These are the basic motions that introduce an item of business before an assembly. Most motions in a church business meeting fall in this class.

2. Restorative motions.—This class of motions "restores" by bringing back for further consideration a motion that was before the assembly and was disposed of in a previous meeting. The motions in this class include: (1) reconsider, (2) rescind or amend something previously adopted, and (3) take from the table.

3. Incidental motions.—These motions are referred to as incidental because they take care of certain procedural matters that arise while handling the business of the meeting. The motions included are: (1) Point of order, (2) Appeal, (3) Parliamentary inquiry, (4) Point of information, (5) Division of the assembly, (6) Division of a question, and (7) Suspend the rules.

4. Subsidiary motions.—These are used to dispose of main motions: (1) Lay on the table, (2) Previous question, (3) Limit or extend debate, (4) Postpone to a certain time, (5) Refer to committee, (6) Amend, and (7) Postpone indefinitely.

5. Privileged motions.—These motions are urgent ones that allow the assembly to interrupt the consideration of anything else. (1) Fix the time for adjournment, (2) Adjourn, (3) Recess, (4)

Question of privilege, and (5) Call for the orders of the day.

Seeing that churches conduct the most important business in the world, your growing knowledge of how these classes of motions operate will enable you to facilitate a church business meeting marked by honor and unity.

Practical pointers for the Moderator

- [ ] The moderator should always embody the spirit of Christ.
- [ ] The meeting should begin on time.
- [ ] The moderator should have copies of all governing documents.
- [ ] The moderator should have a copy of the minutes and review them before meeting.
- [ ] The moderator should have a copy of all recommendations and review them before the meeting.
- [ ] The moderator should adhere to the agenda for the meeting.
- [ ] The moderator should remain impartial in all matters under discussion and relinquish the chair if he/she feels the need to engage in the discussion.
- [ ] The moderator treats every member the same.
- [ ] The moderator seeks to help the member do what they are trying to do.

Decorum and Debate

✓ Every member should embody the spirit of Christ and remember that "a soft answer turneth away wrath."

✓ No one speaks without first standing and being recognized by the chair.

✓ All remarks are to be addressed to and through the chair.

✓ No discussion is permitted until a motion has been made, seconded (if required), and stated by the chair.

✓ The maker of a motion has the privilege of speaking first.

✓ After the maker of a motion speaks, the debate then alternates between those for and against the motion.

✓ After speaking once to a motion, you may not speak again until everyone wishing to speak has spoken and after speaking a second time, you may not address that subject again.

✓ In all discussion, remarks are always confined to the merits of the proposal and never are allowed to focus on persons, personalities, or motives.

Some Final Words of Wisdom

▪ Never hesitate to say, "I'm sorry. I was wrong."

▪ It is not your church.

- Committees solve problems. Meetings approve solutions.
- A bulldog can whip a skunk, but it's not worth it.
- You don't have to win every battle to win the war.
- Patience will gain more than haste.
- People are more important than procedures.
- You cannot take an organization where it does not want to go.
- Tell the truth and trust the people.
- If you continue doing things the way that you have always done them, things will continue being what they have always been!

Practical Application Exercises

1. Interview three ministers who are currently serving in churches.
   a. Write down this information from each interview:
      i. Does your church still have business meetings?
      ii. Who serves as the moderator during the business meetings?
      iii. What is the quorum required for the regular business meeting?
      iv. Who can call for the special business meeting?

    b. Prepare a summation of 1,000 words or fewer comparing the answers to the interview with the information presented in this chapter.

2. Write a handout on parliamentary procedure in which you define and summarize the rules for conducting effective meetings in the church.

3. Identify the five lines of authority for conducting church meetings.

Recommended Resources for Further Study

Lochrie, James, <u>Meeting Procedures: Parliamentary Law and Rules of Order for the 21st Century</u>. Scarecrow Press, 2003. (ISBN 978-0-585-45986-8)

McCarty, C. Barry, <u>A Parliamentary Guide for Church Leaders</u>. B&H Publishing Group, 2012. (ISBN 978-1-433-67737-3)

Merrill, R. Dale, <u>The Church Business Meeting</u>. Judson Press, 1968. (ISBN 978-0-817-00409-5)

Noyce, Gaylord, <u>Church Meetings That Work</u>. Wipf & Stock Publishers, 2012. (ISBN 978-1-620-32800-2)

Olsen, Charles M., Transforming Church Boards Into Communities of Spiritual Leaders. Alban Institute, 1995. (ISBN 978-1-566-99148-3)

Trohan, Colette Collier, A Great Meeting Needs a Great Secretary! A Great Meeting, Inc., 2015. (ISBN 978-0-976-88058-5)

Administering Church Discipline

It is difficult to imagine what it would be like to live in a society where citizens could flaunt the rules and absolutely no consequences would follow—no fines, no imprisonment, etc. Can you conceive of a home environment where the children are allowed to do whatever they please with utterly no discipline imposed? Total chaos would reign in either of these instances.

Yet there are countless congregations belonging to Jesus Christ across our nation where little, if any, discipline of the wayward is ever enacted. Is it any wonder that our brotherhood is weaker today than it has been in decades?

Exactly, what is church discipline? In its broadest sense, it involves everything from the most basic instruction that the new-born child of God receives—from the time of his conversion onward, all the way to the radical "surgery" sometimes required in the withholding of fellowship from impenitent apostates.

The first thing that we must realize is that church discipline is for the purpose of restoring the wayward Christian—not just getting rid of him or her. If a Christian will not repent of sin, then he or she should be removed from the church membership, but that is not what we should desire. We should desire restoration.

Church discipline starts out one on one. If you see a fellow Christian that is committing a sin, then you should go to that one alone. Many people run right to the Pastor, or to one of the deacons and say, "Say, do you know what ____ is doing? He is doing a terrible thing!" That is not the right way to handle a problem. If we see someone committing a sin, then we should make sure that we are right with God ourselves, and then pray about the matter, and then go to the person alone.

New Testament Authority for Discipline

Every serious Bible student knows that there is ample authority for the practice of church discipline. Consider the following samples of New Testament evidence:

1. Jesus taught that one who has wronged his brother, and who cannot persuaded to repent—either by the offended party, other independent witnesses, or the church in general—should be treated as the Gentile and the publican (Matthew 18:17). In the context of a first-century setting, this means that the church was to have no social contact with hardened offenders.

2. Paul instructed the saints in Rome to be on the lookout for those who are causing the divisions and occasions of stumbling contrary to the doctrine. He declared that the faithful should turn away from these self-serving egotists who were deceiving the innocent (Romans 16:17).

3. The entire fifth chapter of 1 Corinthians deals with the matter of discipline. A fornicating church member had pursued in his immoral lifestyle relentlessly, and the apostle rebuked the Corinthian congregation for not having withheld fellowship from the man. Paul declared the brother should have been taken away from among you, delivered unto Satan, and put away (vv. 2, 5, 13). Further, with such a one, company was not to be kept. The fraternization of a common meal was forbidden (v. 11). This instruction is quite explicit.

4. The inspired Paul commanded the church Thessalonica to withdraw from every brother who persists in walking disorderly, thus contrary to divinely received traditions (2 Thessalonians 3:6). Such persons, says he, are to be identified and social company with them is to be severed. Excommunicated brethren, of course, are not to be treated harshly; rather, they are to be admonished in a brotherly fashion (vv. 14, 15; cf. Galatians 6:1).

5. In Titus 3:10, inspiration affirms that a factious person, after appropriate admonition, is to be refused, i.e., refused further association.

These passages by no means exhaust the New Testament information on the subject of church discipline. They are sufficient, however, to provide ample instruction of the kingdom's responsibility in this regard.

The Purpose of Church Discipline

What is the purpose in withdrawing fellowship from the disorderly? It certainly is not an act of revenge toward those who have fallen from the faith. And it must never be exercised in a haughty or malevolent manner. The Scriptures do suggest, however, that discipline has both a corrective and a protective function.

Obviously, it is designed to save the erring child of God. The Corinthian fornicator was to be removed from the fellowship so that he might be motivated to destroy the flesh, i.e., his ungodly fleshly passion in order that his spirit might be saved in the day of the Lord Jesus (1 Corinthians 5:5). Discipline is designed to gain the wayward (Matthew 18:15), to make him ashamed (2 Thessalonians 3:14), to the end that he may be restored (Galatians 6:1).

A consideration of certain passages in 2 Corinthians leads to the conclusion that the church in Corinth finally did withdraw from the sensuous offender, and that such brought him to repentance (2:6).

But discipline is not merely for the welfare of the rebel. It is for the protection of the church as well.

When Paul admonished the congregation at Corinth to take care of the problem of the immoral brother, he warned: "Don't you know that a little leaven leavens the whole lump?" (1 Corinthians 5:6). The apostles elsewhere declared that those who cause divisions and occasions of stumbling by their smooth and fair speech beguile the hearts of the innocent (Romans 16:17).

Two false teachers in the early church, Hymenaeus and Alexander, had made shipwreck of the faith, hence Paul delivered them unto Satan, i.e., he withdraw fellowship from them (1 Timothy 1: 19-20; cf. 1 Corinthians 5:5) for the welfare of the brethren. False teaching, if allowed to go unchecked within the body of Christ, can eat like a cancer and cause the faith of some to be overthrown (see 2 Timothy 2:16-18).

Discipline is also important in preserving the integrity of the church before the eyes of the world. Society has bias enough against us without having the legitimate complaint that we harbor evil within our fellowship. We should never give occasion to the adversary for reviling (1 Timothy 5:14).

It is imperative that the conduct of the church be such that the name of God and the doctrine not be blasphemed (1 Timothy 6:1), and that the way of truth be not evil spoken of (2 Peter 2:2).

Conduct Deserving of Church Discipline

What sort of attitude or conduct warrants the extreme measure of withdrawing fellowship? The Bible addresses this matter in several ways:

1. A brother who has sinned against another, but who refuses to repent of his transgression, could ultimately be removed from the fellowship (Matthew 18:15-17).

2. Those who cause occasions of stumbling and who initiate division are proper subjects for church discipline (Romans 16:17; Titus 3:10).

3. Those who are practitioners of such sins as fornication, covetousness, extortion, idolatry, drunkenness, reviling, etc., could certainly be candidates for withdrawal (1 Corinthians 5:9ff).

4. Advocates of soul-threatening doctrines must not be allowed to continue in open fellowship with the church (1 Timothy 1:19-20; 2 Timothy 2:16-18).

5. Those who walk disorderly are to be refused association by the faithful (2 Thessalonians 3:6). But what is disorderly conduct? There are those who simply grow weary of the Christian life and decide to resign from the church. When approached about their neglect, and warned of possible discipline, they raise a voice of protest, claiming: "What am I doing that is wrong? I am not committing adultery; I am not a drunkard. The church cannot withdraw from me." An appropriate response would be: "Are you faithfully serving God? Do you meet with your brethren to sing, pray, observe the Lord's Supper, etc.? What would be the fate of the

family of God if every member were at liberty to do as you have done?" Spiritual neglect is disorderly conduct, and a fitting response to such is discipline—of some sort at least.

It would be well to remember, however, that a person's disposition is frequently the determining factor in terms of when, or whether, withdrawal of fellowship should be administered. No wise church leadership would withdraw fellowship hastily a sincere Christian who, through weakness, had fallen into a sinful situation. As long as there is humility on the part of the offender, and a genuine effort to overcome the problem, long-suffering would be indicated. When, though, a surly, rebellious attitude is evidenced, more drastic measures may be speedily indicated.

Faithful elderships should let it be known that if a person wants to identify with the congregation over which they exercise supervision, he or she will be expected to live right, and to assume a healthy responsibility in the areas of Christian growth and service. If there is remiss in these matters, discipline, in some form or another, could be advisable.

How Should the Final Act Be Administered?

In every congregation where qualified men are serving as elders, it naturally would be the case that the eldership would lead the church in the withdrawal of fellowship from the unfaithful. Let it be stressed, however, that disfellowship is not an eldership act behind closed doors. It is an activity on the part of the entire church, and the formalization of the procedure must be enacted in the public assembly.

Paul commands the Corinthian Christians, by the authority of Christ, to deliver the erring brother unto Satan when they are gathered together (1 Corinthians 5:4). Similarly, after the Lord gave instructions regarding the procedures for restoring the brother who had wronged his fellow, he declared: "For where two or three are gathered together in my name, there am I in the midst of them" (Matthew 18:20).

Few people seem to recognize that this comforting promise is given within a context of an exhortation regarding church discipline. Lenski has well noted that Christ is in the assembly of the church or present when two or three are convicting a brother of sin, it is he himself who acts with his church and its members when they carry out his Word by invoking also his presence and his help.

Objections to Church Discipline—Answered

In spite of the fact that the Bible is quite clear on the obligation of Christ's church to practice discipline upon impenitent members, there are those who cavil against the responsibility—even to the point of asserting that withdrawal of fellowship is a violation of New Testament principles. Some of the more common quibbles offered are:

"No one is worthy to disfellowship another."

The allegation is sometimes made that since no one is perfect, no one really has the right to initiate discipline against another. Commonly, John 8:7 will be cited as a proof-text for this idea: "He that is without sin among you, let him first cast a stone at her." Such is a woeful misuse of this passage. Two points need to be noted.

First, the Jews had brought a woman to Christ whom they claimed to have taken in the very act of adultery. They wanted the Lord to sanction her death (thus involving him in difficulty with the Roman authorities). However, though the Old Testament law had clearly stated that both parties in an adulterous union must be executed, these Jews had brought only the woman. Hence, they had ignored the very law they pretended to honor.

Christ's statement, therefore, as quoted above, was designed to highlight this inconsistency. It cannot be employed to militate against plain commands obligating the church to discipline the wayward.

Second, Paul was not without sin, and yet, he withdrew himself from evil brethren (1 Timothy 1:19, 20). One does not have to be sinless in order to honor the Bible teaching on this vital theme.

"Leave the tares for God."

It sometimes is contended that whereas it must be acknowledged that there are tares in the kingdom, we are instructed to leave them alone. At the judgment, the Lord will exercise his own discipline (cf. Matthew 13:24-30, 36-43).

In response, we must insist that no parabolic teaching can be arrayed against clear Bible instruction given elsewhere. This argument is like suggesting that simply because the debtor (in the parable of the unmerciful servant) was forgiven by his Lord, with no conditions being stated (Matthew 18:27), one may conclude that salvation is totally unconditional!

The parable of the tares is simply designated to inoculate against violent and premature attempts to completely purify the church on earth. It has nothing to do with the genuine practice of brotherly discipline. J. W. McGarvey noted that this type of reasoning is in direct conflict with the teaching of both Jesus and the apostles on the subject of withdrawing from the disorderly.

"Judge not!"

Some contend that church discipline would be a form of judging, a practice which the Bible condemns. The plain truth is, not all judging is wrong!

Jesus declared: "Judge not according to appearance, but judge ye righteous judgment" (John 7:24). In Paul's rebuke of the Corinthians, he clearly stated that he had judged already the incestuous brother (1 Corinthians 5:3). He then subsequently asked these brethren, "Do not ye judge them that are within?" (5:12). Church discipline does, therefore, involve a form of judging, but it is not the unjustified, hypocritical judgment that is censured by Christ in Matthew 7:1-5).

"Where is the love?"

It is sometimes charged that if the church withdraws fellowship from the erring, it is demonstrating a lack of love. The sickening, superficial view that so many have regarding love these days is one of the most dramatic commentaries on biblical ignorance.

The fact is, discipline does not repudiate love it reflects love: "Those whom the Lord loves, he disciplines" (Hebrews 12:6, NASB). When ancient Israel went astray, Jehovah withdrew his presence from them for seventy years (the Babylonian captivity). Was this an indication of an unloving disposition? To even suggest such is blasphemous.

If you are a member of a congregation which practices church discipline, you ought to thank Almighty God that you have the privilege of belonging to such a loving family!

"What about him?"

Occasionally the claim will be made: "The church cannot withdraw from me, for there are others who are just as bad, or worse, and they haven't been disciplined." Several things may be said in rebutting this rationalization.

First, the fact that the church may have been remiss in this duty, or even inconsistent, in the past, does not mean that changes for the better cannot be made. No sane person would argue: "We were wrong in the past; let us therefore always be wrong."

Second, the precise determination as to whom, and when, church discipline should be administered will frequently be a matter of leadership judgment. Some brethren may not know all the facts as to why decisions were made to withdraw from some and not from others. There may be extenuating circumstances that are not general information. This type of quibbling cannot be allowed to deter discipline when such is obviously indicated.

Loving discipline was as much a trait of the primitive church as correct worship, organization, etc. This question, then, cannot but haunt many: can a church that utterly refuses to practice discipline truly be a New Testament church?

Practical Application Exercises

1. Write a summation of 1,000 words or fewer detailing the need for effective church administration.

2. Write a paragraph in 750 words or slightly less, in which you define church administration.

Recommended Resources for Further Study

Adams, Jay E., Handbook of Church Discipline. Zondervan, 1986. (ISBN 978-0-310-51191-5)

Adams, Jay E., How to Help People Change: The Four-Step Biblical Process. Zondervan, 2010. (ISBN 978-0-310-87706-6)

Laney, J. Carl, A Guide to Church Discipline: God's Loving Plan for Restoring Believers to Fellowship with Himself and with the Body of Christ. Wipf and Stock Publishers, 2010. (ISBN 978-1-608-99452-6)

Leeman, Jonathan, Church Discipline: How the Church Protects the Name of Jesus: Crossway, 2012. (ISBN 978-1-433-53236-8)

MacArthur, John, The Freedom and Power of Forgiveness. Crossway, 2009. (ISBN 978-1-433-52395-3)

White, John & Blue, Ken, <u>Healing the Wounded: the Costly Love of Church Discipline</u>. Intervarsity Press, 1985. (ISBN 978-0-877-84939-1)

I – Sample Covenant between Pastor & Church

(A covenant between the Pastor and the Church is a good document to have in place at the beginning of a new call because it clearly outlines and details the roles and responsibilities of each party to the other in addition to agreements made during the initiating of the call.)

1. The Pastor's Responsibility to the Church

1.01 To proclaim the gospel with the goal of reaching persons for Christ and fostering academic, emotional, social, and spiritual growth.

1.02 To love and affirm persons and families within the fellowship without bias or prejudice.

1.03 To provide counseling to members and non-members and to keep confidential such communication.

1.04 To serve as administrator of church programs and ministries by facilitating communication and recommending appropriate ministries/programs to the appropriate persons.

1.05 To work with committees, organizations, and boards in the development and implementation of programs of ministry and mission. Chairpersons of committees, organizations, and boards are to have the responsibility of their offices with the counsel of the pastor as desired or needed. All committees, organizations, and boards are ultimately responsible to the church from which their authority is derived and their responsibilities are defined.

1.06   To be ex officio member of all committees with exception of the personnel committee, the diaconate, and the diaconate election committee. (The pastor's counsel shall be sought concerning other staff.) The pastor shall, as a member of said committees, offer expertise and advice but shall not be entitled to vote.

1.07   To give primary oversight and direct the church office, supervising the church secretary, overseeing that the church calendar is maintained, representing the church to visitors and other persons who might come in contact with the church, advising other church members of information they need to carry out their duties as church officers, and serving in other reasonable activities relative to the church office.

1.08   To establish church office hours and generally seek to maintain those office hours for the benefit of all church members and the related business of the church; in times of absence, the church secretary should be informed as to how to contact the pastor.

1.09 To visit the sick, the elderly, and the bereaved and to maintain contact with the membership as a whole.

1.10 To be an encourager to persons, programs, and ministries of the church family.

1.11 To be actively involved in and supportive of the local Baptist association, the Louisiana Baptist Convention and the denomination in its work and ministries.

2.   The Church's Responsibility to the Pastor

a.   To show sensitivity to the physical, spiritual, and emotional needs of the pastor and family.

b.   To pray for the pastor's ministry, affirm efforts, and work with the pastor toward the end of accomplishing God's will in the church and the community.

c.   To allow the pastor full responsibility for the preaching program of the church with privilege of calling on others for participation.

d.   To allow the pastor responsibility for the administration of the ordinances of baptism and the Lord's Supper as shared in the fellowship and to receive new members and assist in their orientation.

e.   To support the pastor in the church's preaching ministry and to cooperate with the pastor by suggesting programs and providing groups such as the deacons to act as a sounding board.

f.   To acknowledge that we are all imperfect human beings seeking to serve a perfect God.

g.   To be willing to inform the pastor of misunderstandings so that wrongs may be righted.

3.   Working Guidelines

a.   A call to serve as pastor will also include a signed covenant agreement that has been read and approved by the members and signed by the deacon chairman or moderator of the church.

b.   The church shall be responsible for insurance on contents of the pastor's study at the church and malpractice insurance as appropriate.

c.   The church will lease a cellphone for use by the pastoral family and the church secretary in contacting the pastor.

d.   The pastor selection committee will meet with the pastor quarterly for evaluation and feedback during the first year of service.

e.   This covenant agreement shall be reviewed annually and renegotiated as necessary. The pastor and congregation must concur on any change.

4.   Employment Guidelines

a.   The pastor is directly responsible to the congregation in the performance of ministry. The pastor shall meet annually with the personnel committee of the church for review and evaluation of ministry. The pastor shall, with the deacons, oversee the pastoral care and nurture of the church members and provide for a continuing, diversified program of ministries among the members.

b.   If the pastor is to be gone overnight from the church field, the pastor shall inform the church secretary as to the location.

c.   The pastor is expected to give the church forty-eight hours of his time during the week and to be on call for emergencies twenty-four hours per day, seven days a week.

d.   If the pastor is to be away for more than thirty-six hours, church leaders should be told how to reach the pastor, or the pastor should provide a qualified person to serve during the absence.

e.   When the pastor is away from the church field for more than three days, the deacons should be made aware so that crises can be covered by other leaders.

f.	The pastor will give the deacons a monthly report on visits, membership and personal needs, and church activities. After particularly strenuous times that demand excessive work hours during the church year, the pastor is encouraged to take time off for rest and relaxation.

g.	The pastor will be allowed three weeks' vacation, including three Sundays.

h.	The pastor is allowed thirty days per year as sick leave with full salary and benefits. For a prolonged illness, continued payment will be at the discretion of the church.

i.	The pastor is allowed two weeks per year for revivals or continuing education; the latter may be paid for from convention expense funds. One week of this may be used for additional vacation time if not needed for revival or continuing education.

j.	The church will provide the pulpit supply in case of illness, bereavement, and vacation. The pastor is responsible for the supply when preaching in revival elsewhere.

## 5.	Financial Care

a.	The church agrees to pay for all moving expenses incurred, including a mover of the pastor's choice. The pastor shall obtain at least two competitive bids for this expense.

b.   The church agrees to allow the pastor to choose and purchase or rent a home or use the church-owned parsonage.

c.   The church agrees to begin the pay period as of the last day of the pay period in the previous church; i.e., July 31/August 1; and the pastor agrees to begin new duties on that same day.

d.   Regular pay periods will fall on the fifteenth and last days of each month.

e.   In case of termination, care will be given to minimize harm to the pastoral family and to the church's witness.

II – Sample Musician/Minister of Music Contract with Church

(The following is a sample contract for use by church musicians. It should be considered as a guide to be adapted to each situation. It includes items of mutual importance and helps eliminate the possibility of future misunderstandings. This contract should be signed by the musician and an officer of the church authorized to do so.)

Effective on (DATE), and until the termination of this agreement as hereinafter provided, (NAME) shall act as (TITLE OF POSITION), at (NAME OF CHURCH) at a salary of $(AMOUNT) per year payable _____. This salary shall be reviewed annually at the time of the preparation of the church budget.

The above named person shall:

1. Provide organ music and direct the choir(s) at the ___ service(s) regularly scheduled on Sunday morning/Saturday afternoon) and shall select appropriate organ and choral music for each service. Also, select hymns and service music in consultation with the minister/pastor.

2. Provide organ and choral music for the following additional services during the year: _____.

---

3. Be responsible for the leadership of the following choirs: _____.

4. Rehearse once weekly (or as otherwise specified) with each of the choirs. During the summer months, the choir schedule shall be: _____.

5. Cooperate with the pastor and/or music/worship/liturgy committee in the area of the general planning and leadership of the music program. The person shall be directly responsible to: (NAME OF COMMITTEE OR TITLE OR PERSON)

6. Be responsible for the purchase of all necessary music and music supplies and the hiring of all instrumental and vocal soloists. Expenditures in this area shall not exceed the amount provided in the church budget. The budget in the coming year for these expenses is: $(AMOUNT).

7. Be permitted to use the church facilities (organ, piano) for private teaching. Times of lessons and use of facilities must be scheduled in advance through the church office so as not to conflict with other church program needs.

8. Provide music at all weddings requiring organ music held within the church. The services of other organists may be used only with the permission of the regular organist. In such cases, the regular organist shall receive his/her normal wedding fee.

For a short program of organ music preceding the wedding ceremony and for performing at the wedding ceremony, the fee shall be $(AMOUNT). For attendance at the wedding rehearsal, an additional fee shall be $(AMOUNT). Additional fees shall apply for special music or if attendance at extra rehearsals is required.

9. Provide music for funeral services held within the church, if available at the time of the funeral. The fee for such a service shall be $(AMOUNT). If unavailable, the organist shall assist in securing the services of a substitute organist.

10. Report to the appropriate committee the condition and needs for the maintenance of the church organ(s) and piano(s). The church shall provide funds for the proper care of these instruments.

11. Be responsible for setting policies regarding the use of the church's musical instruments.

12. Give notice of termination of employment at least sixty (60) days in advance of the termination.

THE CHURCH SHALL:

13. Provide a vacation (with full salary) of ___ weeks annually. (The musician will assist the church in obtaining a substitute.) The church shall pay for the services of a substitute organist and/or director.

14. Grant up to __ weeks (__weekly rehears-als/___services) sick leave during the year. In the case of extended illness, the church should consid-er the granting of additional sick leave time.

15. Provide the following essential benefits for the above-named person and their family: Blue Cross/Blue Shield (or similar health plan), major medical insurance, Social Security, pension plan, disability and life insurance. These benefits shall take into account the person's needs and be com-mensurate with the benefits received by other employees of the church.

16. Reimburse the above named person up to $(amount) annually, for expenses incurred by the person in attending a church music conference, workshop or institute, or other forms of continuing education.

Give sixty (60) days advance notice if they wish to terminate employment.

III – Annual Itemized Contribution Statement for Tax Purposes

(The following is an example of an Annual Contribution Statement. It can be detailed or as simple as you desire as long as it contains these ...

5 Essential Elements:

1. *Organization's name*
2. *Donor's name*
3. *Date(s) of contribution(s)*
4. *Amount(s) of contribution(s)*
5. *A statement explaining whether the charity provided any goods or services to the donor for the contribution. If no goods or services were provided, you would include similar wording such as: 'You did not receive any goods or services in connection with these contributions other than intangible religious benefits'.)*

Dear [personalize],

We thank God for you! Your gifts to _____ Church throughout [year] are gratefully acknowledged.

Because of your contributions, our congregation has been able to support the work of Jesus Christ locally, regionally, and around the world. *(Briefly mention some examples of what the church was able to do in missions and ministry during the previous year.)*

Attached *(or "Here" if a short list...just list below)* is an itemized statement of your contributions for [year], according to our records. If you have any concerns about the accuracy of this information, please let us know.

For income tax purposes, it is important for us to state here that you did not receive any goods or services in return for any of these contributions other than intangible religious benefits. You made these gifts out of your own generosity and commitment to Jesus Christ.

{Whether you insert or omit this next paragraph is totally up to you. Some might find it too pushy...while others may feel that a gentle reminder is a good idea.}

Our records show that you pledged ____ for the year and paid ___ of that pledge. (*If the pay up is not complete, you may wish to include sentences like these: "Although the books are closed for [year], if you are able to do so you are invited to consider fulfilling last year's pledge along with this year's commitment. Of course gifts to the church will be deductible in the year they are given."*)

Once again, thank you for your generous commitment to the work of Jesus Christ through this church.

Sincerely,

Your Name
Church Title
Dated

IV – Noncash Contribution Receipt

(The following is an example of a receipt you would grant to someone for making a noncash contribution to your church. In this example, the item donated is a printer for the church business office.)

Dear [personalize],

Thank you for your contribution of a HP color Deskjet printer in good condition.

You did not receive any goods or services in connection with this contribution other than intangible religious benefits.

If you plan on claiming a tax deduction for this contribution you are responsible for establishing the value of the donated item. If the value of the item exceeds $500 you will be required to file Form 8283. If the value exceeds $5,000 you may be required to obtain a certified appraisal. Consult your tax preparer for additional details.

Once again, thank you for your generous commitment to the work of Jesus Christ through this church.

Sincerely,

Your Name
Church Title
Dated

V – Church Membership Transfer Letter

(The Membership Transfer letter for churches is used when a church receives a request or needs to transfer membership from one church to another church. The sample transfer letter form is a final decision for the Church Board and Pastor to make before sending the Membership Transfer letter to the church gaining membership.)

To the [Name of church requesting letter] Church in [City, State]:

This certifies that [Member's Name] is a member in good standing of the [Name of church granting letter] Church in [City, State] and at [his/her] request is transferred and is affectionately recommended to your fellowship.

If notified within six months of [his/her] union with you, we shall consider [him/her] as transferred from us; otherwise this letter shall be null and void.

On behalf of the Church.

_____   _____
Church Clerk   Date

_____
Pastor

VI – Inactive Membership Letter

(This letter is a sample that can easily be used when a member(s) makes a decision to leave the church for whatever reason and becomes inactive. This letter is a way of letting your inactive member(s) know that they will be missed and will always be welcomed back as an active member if they decide to do so.)

Dear [Member],

Your home church cherishes you as a member of this fellowship. We have sought to mediate the privileges and blessings which we have in association together in the [Church Name] Church. The hallowed fellowship, the helpfulness, the watch care and counsel are very sacred and precious.

However, according to our records, you have been absent from religious services for at least six successive months, and have not responded to the encouragement to be active when possible. Therefore, the Church Board has placed your name on the roll of inactive membership on [date]. This action does not remove you from our prayers and concern. Any time you call we will seek to minister to you faithfully as the church has done in the past. Inactive members are not eligible to vote in church meetings or to hold church office, but we encourage you not to lose touch with the fellowship.

We believe things will change for you and you will be interested in becoming active in your church again. When that happens, you may request to be returned to the active roll, and upon reaffirmation of the vows of membership and renewed participation in the worship activities of this local church, this may be done. The Church Board will respond to such a request within 60 days.

May you feel God's grace and love and that of the love of your church family too.

Yours in Christ,

Your Name
Title
Dated

Bibliography

Buntain, Fulton W., The Pentecostal Pastor. Gospel Publishing House, 2008.

Burroughs, P. E., Honoring the Deaconship. Sunday School Board, 1929.

Carter, Homer D., Equipping Deacons in Caring Skills. Convention Press, 1980.

Dargan, E. C., Ecclesiology: A Study of the Churches. Chas. T. Dearing, 1897.

Flake, Floyd, African American Church Management Handbook. The Judson Press, 2005.

Foshee, Howard B., The Ministry of the Deacon. Convention Press, 1968.

Heath, Chip & Dan. Made to Stick: Why Some Ideas Survive and Others Die. Random House, 2007.

Lenski, R. C. H., The Interpretation of St. Matthew's Gospel, Augsburg, 1961.

Malphurs, Aubrey, Ministry Nuts and Bolts: What They Don't Teach Pastors in Seminary. Kregel Publications, 2009.

McGarvey, J. W., <u>Commentary on Matthew and Mark</u>. Eugene Smith, n.d.

McNamara, Roger N., <u>How to Write a Church Constitution</u>. Baptist Mid-Missions, 2006.

Naylor, Robert E., <u>The Baptist Deacon</u>. Broadman Press, 1955.

Nichols, Harold, <u>The Work of the Deacons and Deaconesses</u>. The Judson Press, 1964.

Robert, Henry M. et al., <u>Robert's Rules of Order Newly Revised (11th ed.)</u>. Da Capo Press, 2011.

Sheffield, Barbara, <u>Help! I'm a Deacon's Wife</u>. Convention Press, 1992.

Sheffield, Robert, <u>The Ministry of Baptist Deacons</u>. Convention Press, 1990.

Thayer, J. H., <u>Greek-English Lexicon of the New Testament</u>. T. & T. Clark, 1958.

Tidwell, Charles A., <u>Church Administration: Effective Leadership for Ministry</u>. Broadman Press, 1985.

Tyson, John H., <u>Administration in the Small Membership Church</u>. Abingdon Press, 2007.

Warren, Rick, <u>The Purpose Driven Church: Every Church is Big in God's Eyes</u>. Zondervan, 1995.

Webb, Henry, <u>Deacons: Servant Models in the Church</u>. Convention Press, 1980.

Other Books:

THE Minister's Handbook:
A Guide for Leadership

Preaching that Empowers God's People:
Expository Preaching in the 21st Century

Conducting Church Audits:
A Guide for Internal Auditors

www.ingramcontent.com/pod-product-compliance
Lightning Source LLC
Chambersburg PA
CBHW021839020426

42334CB00014B/707